Developing an IT strategy for your library

Alec Gallimore

Central Library Manager,
Manchester Central Library

Library Association Publishing
London

Published by
Library Association Publishing
7 Ridgmount Street
London WC1E 7AE

Library Association Publishing is wholly owned by The Library Association.

First published 1997

British Library Cataloguing in Publication Data
A catalogue record for this book is available from the British Library

ISBN 1-85604-261-8

Typeset in 11/13pt Century Schoolbook and Oranda by Library Association Publishing.
Printed and made in Great Britain by Bookcraft (Bath) Ltd.

Contents

5 Internal audit 51

6 The external context 70

7 Elements of the strategy – physical infrastructure 88

8 Elements of the strategy – policy and management 110

9 Evaluation and implementation 128

10 Monitoring and review 155

Introduction

Get IT sorted

IT is developing rapidly on many different fronts. Changes in software and hardware, changes in networking and services, changes in media and access to information are creating a complex mix of possibilities, threats and opportunities for all libraries. Librarians may feel that they are being buried beneath an avalanche of new technology. There is an unfamiliar language to learn which is constantly changing. The learning curve for new technology seems to grow steeper all the time.

Frequent questions are: Where do we begin? Where is it taking us? How do we keep up? Which trend should we follow? How can we find the money for IT? How will we implement new systems? Will staff be able to cope? What do the users really want?

To avoid the feeling that the technology is in control there is a need to take control of the technology.

To do this it is essential to develop a clear IT strategy, concentrating on the strategic use of IT systems as part of the overall management strategy of the library service.

The strategy development process

This book seeks to provide a detailed map of the process of developing an IT strategy, from the initial research to the final implementation. The process has been outlined in a convenient form which can be picked up and followed by any library or information service with a minimum of adaptation.

Aims of the book

The main purpose of the book is to provide guidance for librarians and information workers who wish to produce an IT strategy for their library or information service. The book draws upon the experience of the author in producing an IT strategy for Manchester Public Libraries and upon the strategies of other organizations.[1] In doing so the book shows how an IT strategy can be developed in a logical and coherent way as part of the overall management strategy of the library or information service, rather than being a series of *ad hoc* IT projects.

The aims of the book are to:

□ show the need for IT strategies in libraries
□ illustrate the benefits of an IT strategy
□ outline the strategy development process
□ produce a clear guide for libraries to design a strategy that avoids a piecemeal approach to IT
□ illustrate the need for a thorough understanding of the internal and external environments
□ outline the physical and management elements of an IT infrastructure
□ map out a plan for implementing IT systems in libraries and for monitoring their effectiveness
□ look at future influences on IT strategy in libraries.

IT is universal. The intention has been to produce a guide relevant to managers in any library or information service, wherever it is situated. Although there may be documents available on IT strategy for other types of organizations, librarians will prefer a text which relates more closely to their own subject field and has been written with an appreciation of common problems and constraints.

What this book does not do

This book does not recommend a single blueprint as an ideal IT strategy. It recognizes that all libraries are different, their needs are different, their levels of resources are different, the circumstances in which they operate are different. Each library will produce a different strategy according to its needs. However, there will be common elements in these strategies and most importantly there is a common process which can be followed in developing an IT strategy.

The book is not meant to be a guide to selecting and installing particular IT systems, nor does it seek to recommend or give advice on specific products. It is concerned with the planning of IT systems rather than the practical aspects of installation and day-to-day running. It is not a technical manual and does not give any detailed descriptions of the working of networks, hardware or software. If this information is needed in the process of research for the strategy it can be found in detail elsewhere.

A step-by-step process

The book has been designed to provide a practical text that can be followed in sequence from beginning to end to produce an IT strategy for a library or information service. The level of detail required for different libraries will vary. Larger services will need to undertake extensive research to assess the many and varied needs of their users and to translate those needs into a workable infrastructure: smaller libraries will benefit from using the process in a less intensive way while still following the basic pattern.

There are checklists throughout the text which will provide convenient reminders of tasks to be undertaken or issues to be considered during the strategy process.

The need for a strategy

Chapter 1 looks at the way changes in society and the rapid growth of IT has made IT strategies essential. Libraries are not alone in seeking to make sense of the effects of the information society upon their services. There are strategies being developed from a global to a local level. These larger strategies will both inform and affect the strategies individual organizations such as libraries adopt. In the global networking culture now evolving, all organizations will be interlinked and their strategies will need to be coherently linked together.

Benefits of a strategy

In Chapter 2 the benefits for a library of developing an IT strategy are outlined.

The basic outline of the strategy process

Chapter 3 provides the basic outline of the strategy development process and gives some information about its different component parts. Successive chapters then provide more detailed steps to follow in designing a strategy which fits into the individual library service's overall management strategy.

Aims and scope of the strategy

Chapter 4 deals with establishing the aims of the strategy and defining its scope before proceeding with the background research.

Internal audit and external factors

Chapter 5 covers the important task of carrying out an internal audit of existing IT systems to assess their future usefulness and their degree of integration with the aims of the library service. The need to establish the context of the library service within the environment in which it operates is covered in Chapter 6. This emphasizes the need for knowledge about the state of the art of IT systems and also the need to have a view of the various pressures acting upon the library service from outside.

The infrastructure

Chapters 7 and 8 deal with planning the necessary IT infrastructure for the library service. Chapter 7 covers the physical elements such as networks, hardware and software and Chapter 8 addresses the important management and policy considerations. The aim is to draw attention to the elements to be considered rather than to prescribe specific solutions. Each library will differ in its needs and its aims and the infrastructure designed will reflect that library service's uniqueness.

Implementation, monitoring and review

In Chapters 9 and 10 the steps to take in producing plans for implementation are outlined, together with ideas for developing monitoring and review procedures to measure the outcomes.

Future strategy

Finally, Chapter 11 deals with the future of IT and libraries. Predicting the future is a dangerous and foolhardy activity and this chapter is not concerned with making specific predictions or drawing up scenarios for the future of library services. The intention is to look at some of the trends that are beginning to emerge now and which are likely to have implications in the near future for IT strategies in libraries.

Reference

1   Gallimore, Alec, 'A public library strategy for the millennium', *Journal of librarianship and information science*, September 1996, 149–57.

1 The need for IT strategies in libraries

Technology . . . the knack of so arranging the world that we need not experience it.

Frisch[1]

Objectives

☐ Show why strategies are needed by libraries to deal with rapid changes in society

☐ Show how strategies are being developed in libraries and other organizations to meet the challenge of the information society.

The effects of IT on libraries
Pressure for change

The changes in society brought about by IT which are occurring with increasing frequency affect all organizations. Libraries cannot ignore the social pressures upon them but must adapt to the changes around them if they are to remain relevant. The changing economy and changes in government policies in the last few years have had a profound effect upon the culture in which organizations operate. Public sector organizations in particular have had to adapt to a period of declining public expenditure, privatization of services and a move from bureaucratic structures to a more open, customer-oriented culture.

The increasing number of older people in the population who are fitter and more active than before, including many people who have retired early and are keen to develop new skills and acquire more knowledge, is leading to a greater demand for flexible education facilities. Libraries need to cater for this increasingly literate and demanding older population.

The increase in part time working and frequent job changes is generating a need for more training, including self-learning using IT packages. The increasing trend of people moving through a portfolio of careers is generating a demand for more accessible information and a need for lifetime learning. Libraries have a major role to play in providing accessible educational facilities.

IT developments are blurring the boundaries between the older institutions. Education need no longer take place in one physical location, information need not be retrieved from a local library, goods and services need not be obtained exclusively from shops in the high street or large supermarkets. Competition exists for the fundamental services which libraries and educational establishments once monopolized.

People now expect the organizations they interact with to use computers. There is a demand for terminal-based access to information from a generation raised on home computers. Remote access to services and teleworking are all adding to the pressure to change the way libraries utilize IT systems.

IT dependency

Libraries and information services like many other organizations are becoming dependent upon IT systems for service delivery, the provision of information, day to day management, administration and communication. Few libraries still have manual issue systems. Those which do have failed to automate largely for financial reasons rather than taking a principled stand against new technology. Earlier, clumsy and slow circulation systems which failed to live up to the promise of increasing productivity have given way to faster, more streamlined systems which provide many more opportunities for library service development. The information handling capabilities of modern systems can be exploited to provide fast retrieval of information for users. The introduction of electronic networking has opened up many more opportunities for service development and improvement.

In the next few years the Internet, Intranets and the concept of networking will play a major role as the next paradigm for change. This will be the era in which IT becomes the backbone of every library. Computer networks will become the structures upon which most organizations will be designed. Communication and information delivery will be the dominant themes. Libraries are changing from being information stores to access points for information retrieval, many are becoming information providers in their own right and taking an active part in the growing global network infrastructure.

The need for IT investment

Investment in IT systems in libraries and other organizations has grown dramatically in recent years. Regular capital investment plans for IT are now essential. The running costs for IT systems have become a significant percentage of the modern organization's overheads.

The cost of installing a network to link up libraries on separate sites with access to central databases and other services can be high. Universities and colleges, particularly in the USA, have invested heavily in connecting their buildings into campus networks, providing network access to staff and students alike. It has become the norm for students to have terminals in their rooms with access to the Internet, e-mail, bulletin boards and to network servers with coursework, information databases and other facilities. Libraries have evolved from being central stores of materials to which every user had to make regular visits and spend many hours in study, to information centres which can distribute information through networks from one end of the world to another. The benefits from investment are therefore being distributed well beyond the physical organization itself.

With networks connecting all organizations in the future, libraries have to consider what their contribution will be to the outside world as well as to their own users. The increasing level of investment needed for an effective IT infrastructure means that local, regional and national cooperation will become essential for future developments.

The need for IT expertise

Although IT expertise is growing within the library and information profession there is still a sharp learning curve for many, especially senior managers who have only lately had to come to terms with new technology. Many of those whose careers have developed through traditional library and information services are reliant upon experts to advise them about IT. The next wave of managers will be expected to be computer-literate in order to make the right decisions for future services.

All staff working in library and information services will need IT skills to operate systems, to help and advise users and to make creative use of increasingly flexible software to develop more specialist services. There is already evidence on the Internet of many new ideas being tested for services through the unifying medium of the world-wide web. A whole new range of skills is being acquired for the development of web pages, interfaces, database access and information delivery.

Implications for libraries

There are many implications for libraries in this growing trend towards IT dependence. Libraries cannot insulate themselves from the process but must adapt to changes in the world around them.

There are implications for:

☐ managing and providing services
☐ internal and external communications
☐ staff training and the skills needed for the effective use of IT
☐ budgets and the provision of increasing revenue costs for IT
☐ capital expenditure for new and replacement equipment
☐ policies for the provision of new IT services to users
☐ making library services accessible on world-wide networks.

The need for strategy

Libraries are taking part in these changes but are often struggling to make sense of the direction the changes are leading to. There is a need to consider carefully the role of the library in this changing world and to map out a clear direction for libraries. Libraries are not alone in needing strategies to deal with the impact of IT and the information society. Strategies are being developed at many levels by governments, international bodies, companies and many other organizations. Libraries should be aware of the impact which these strategies will have upon their own direction in the future.

Strategies for the information society

Information society policies

Strategic planning and policymaking for IT is being explored on many levels, from an all-encompassing global perspective down through continent-wide strategies, national governments, local authorities, multinational companies, universities and educational institutions, libraries, health services, even down to small businesses and other organizations. The need for a strategic approach is seen at every level.

There have been calls for a global strategy for dealing with the benefits and problems associated with IT developments. Libraries have been singled out as intermediaries in the process of bringing the benefits of the information society to the public.

The UNESCO Public Library Manifesto (1994) identified among its 12 key missions: 'Ensuring access for citizens to all sorts of community information; Providing adequate information services to local enterprises, associations and interest groups; Facilitating the development of information and computer literacy skills.'[2] The European Union has recognized the importance of the IT revolution. The formation of partnerships with libraries and other organizations in European countries to bid for development grants is one of the results of this. The European Commission in its 4th Framework Telematics programme (DG XIII 1993) provided specific funding for electronic library projects with the aim of developing library services throughout Europe to meet the demands of the information society.[3] A further 5th Framework programme has been announced.

National strategies

Many countries have now produced national strategies for the information society. Denmark is an example of a country which has produced a strategy which establishes a set of aims for the year 2000.[4] In the section on libraries the principle is stated that: 'Even in the future – where electronic publications will be taking over the role of the magazines and the book – the libraries must maintain a central, intermediate function as providers of all published information for all citizens and in helping to navigate through an increasing flood of information'. In the UK the recent green paper A Prospectus for the Electronic Delivery of

Government Services is an example of the government's approach to strategy on IT.[5] The document refers a number of times to strategy and strategic directions. The fundamental aims are to: 'provide better and more efficient services to business and citizens; improve the efficiency and openness of government administration; and secure substantial cost savings for the taxpayer'.

There are seven main principles outlined in the document to which the strategy seeks to conform.

These are:

☐ choice
☐ confidence
☐ accessibility
☐ efficiency
☐ rationalization
☐ open information
☐ fraud prevention.

Although the document falls short of a national strategy on IT it does indicate that the government has seen the need for a strategy and has provided one interpretation of what a strategy should be. It also gives a view into the future of the delivery of public services via electronic interactive services using public access terminals and the Internet.

The Central Computer and Telecommunications Agency or CCTA has been acting as the main government body in the UK for developing awareness of the implications of the information superhighway and has produced a report on its activities.[6] It has established a Web site at **www.open.gov.uk** which contains links to government departments. Although there is no single definitive government strategy document there are many documents on the subject of the information society at the web site which give an indication of government policies.

A more detailed and considered report from the House of Lords gives a comprehensive overview of the national strategy towards the information society and includes some well-considered comments about public and national libraries, including several recommendations.[7] Among these is: 'a nationally coordinated initiative to enable the benefits of the information superhighway to be delivered using public libraries be developed and supported by Government as part of the Information Society Initiative'. A review of the public libraries in England published by the Department of National Heritage, stressed the importance of the development of electronic networking capabilities between library services across the country and the increasing use of IT for service delivery.[8] However, funding for such developments was only promised after the year 2000.

Local strategies

Some local authorities have well developed strategies for IT development, others have none. There are a few examples in the public domain of published strategies mainly from local authorities in the USA. Christchurch City Council in New Zealand in partnership with Delft and Phoenix is undertaking an international research study to identify the best practices in the use of IT for the strategic management of local government.[9]

Many public libraries have close links with local voluntary groups and some are beginning to cooperate in the development of electronic community information systems. In Manchester, the public library has formed a limited company in conjunction with the Citizens Advice Bureau, a national firm of management consultants, local voluntary groups and city council departments to establish the Manchester Community Information Network (MCIN).[10] The project is designed to provide community information through public terminals in the form of World Wide Web pages which are stored on the Manchester Host, a local Internet provider. Netscape software on the local terminal is used to browse the pages. The Host also provides access through the web pages to local databases. Manchester Public Library's web page, for example, provides access to INFORM, its database of Manchester groups and societies which can be searched using keywords. The facility is also available to all users of the Internet at **http://www.poptel.org.uk/MCIN/**

IT strategies in libraries

National libraries

Several national libraries have produced strategies for the future. The most ambitious plans are probably those of the Library of

Congress which has begun a digitization programme of American historical collections. The Biliothèque Nationale de France also has plans for extensive digital collections of books and images. The British Library has published its own Information Systems Strategy.[11] The strategy includes cooperation with other national libraries around the world in formal and informal agreements, such as CoBRA, the Computerized Bibliographic Record Actions, an EU-funded programme. The strategy compares the situation when the report was written with that expected in the year 2000 and lists a number of objectives which are intended to move the library forward. Among these are improved access to collections through better information, digitization programmes and the establishment of an IT infrastructure to deliver services. National libraries are now working cooperatively to share information and experience in IT developments with a number of specific joint projects already started.

University libraries

Universities in the UK have recently recognized the need for strategies to deal with IT and information. The Follett report recommendations which were adopted by JISC, the Joint Information Systems Committee, in 1993 provided the basis for the development of strategies for dealing with information and its associated technology in higher education.[12]

In the uncertain world of change which all organizations have to operate in there is no single vision for libraries. Neither public libraries nor university libraries can be certain of their role in the future. MacColl reports that more than half of the university libraries in the UK have now been merged with computing services in recognition of the importance of utilizing the expensive campus networks which are being installed as the most effective way of delivering a wide range of information.[13] The Information Strategies Steering Group of JISC has been established to oversee the production of information strategies at a number of pilot sites. Such has been the pressure to conform to this requirement that some have admitted making up strategies simply to keep the funding council quiet. Cooper's and Lybrand were commissioned to produce guidelines on the development of information strategies for universities.[14]

Public libraries

Public libraries have suddenly woken up to the fact that an IT revolution is taking place which could easily leave them marginalized, if not fossilized, in an ever-diminishing role as museums of ancient printed materials. In the USA the Benton Foundation survey has highlighted the dilemma of public libraries which have high public esteem as traditional centres for collections of printed materials and community activity, a view which may hold them back from developing their services in a digital future.[15] The explosion of alternative information sources has forced many public librarians to re-examine their role and the way in which traditional budgets are being stretched in too many directions. Few strategies have been produced to deal with this situation but many libraries have introduced a range of IT systems, often as a result of a desire not to be left behind rather than as a result of systematic planning. Public libraries in the UK, unlike the universities which have JANET and SuperJANET, have no common network linking them together and, because they are controlled by local authorities with different local policies and widely differing levels of funding, there are wide variations in IT development between them.

Cooperative agreements

More and more libraries are seeing the need to cooperate in the development of IT projects, to pool expertise and to bid for external funding. Project Earl has been established to set up web pages and to encourage networking among public libraries. CALIM, the Consortium of Academic Libraries in Manchester, has been successful in attracting funding for a number of projects to develop electronic networking of information between libraries. Of equal importance has been the development of common policies and standards for electronic information and its use among the libraries. CALIM has been involved in the establishment of the GMING broadband backbone project which links the main academic sites in Manchester as well as business organizations and the City Council.

Some IT strategies have been produced by university and public libraries and by other information services. Universities have begun to develop IT and IS strategies to deal with the need to respond to rapid changes in technology which affect the content of nearly every course. Graduates must be up to date with the latest systems and software if they are to keep pace with the demands of employers. Public libraries are also beginning to look seriously at the need to develop strategies. An IT strategy has been produced recently for Manchester Public Libraries in recognition of the need for longer term planning for the introduction of IT systems to meet the future demands of the service.[16] This was approved by Chief Officers and Members in the City Council and is now updated annually. The strategy outlines the library's plan for two to three years ahead, but is regularly reviewed to keep up with changes in technology and the opportunities which arise from new products and techniques.

Many commercial organizations have produced their own IS strategies and some consulting firms provide ready made packages and models for companies to adopt. There is a growing trend for all libraries to produce IT strategy statements to inform staff, users and the wider public about their intentions. Most of these strategies are internal documents and are never published. In order to produce workable strategies library managers would need to search hard to find examples of good practice to follow when designing their own IT strategies. Strategies are, by their nature, highly individualized. What is relevant to one library service may not be relevant to another.

Connectivity

In preparing an IT strategy every library or information service must be aware of the need to connect with other services. If there is one common thread to all IT strategies it is the need for networking between libraries. Whatever local differences there may be, any systems installed should be flexible, open and capable of interconnection with other networks. Only by doing this can libraries ensure that they will have a role to play in the information society of the future.

IT strategy versus information strategy

Information

The most important component of IT is information rather than technology. Information has come to be seen as the fundamental currency of human activity. Phrases such as the information society have become acceptable in everyday usage. The information revolution has replaced the Industrial Revolution as the new wave of human activity in the twentieth century. This emphasis on information has led some commentators to put forward the view that information strategies should be the main concern for organizations. The vogue among commercial organizations is that information systems strategies or IS strategies, which focus on the computer systems which are designed to cope with information should be the main consideration, rather than the technology. However, it is only since the appearance of flexible, easy to use and effective information technology that the information component has become the subject of so much concern.

Information, IS and IT strategies

There is undoubtedly a relationship between information strategy, IS strategy and IT strategy. This might be defined as a triangular model with the main components as the three apexes of the triangle. At different times the three components – information, systems and technology – may have varying levels of importance. All three must be considered in developing a strategy. Although this book is primarily concerned with IT strategy it recognizes that information and systems are equally important considerations. An IT strategy must not be entirely technology driven. It must not simply end up as a wish list of new systems. Instead of looking for ways of using technology within the library service the IT strategy must start by looking at the library service's needs for and uses of information.

Organizational strategy

The main theme of the book is that an IT strategy must be seamlessly linked to the overall strategic aims of the library service. Some multinational companies have realigned their businesses around IT systems in the belief that information rather than their physical products is their major asset. Only by having effective control of their information processes and exploiting the unique information they are generating can companies maintain a competitive edge over others.

For libraries and information services information is their reason for existence so it is all the more important that they should treat information as their most strategic asset. Information technology can no longer be seen simply as an addition to the existing range of services but must be viewed as the central backbone of the library service. An IT strategy is thus essential for making the most effective use of information assets in the library.

References

1 Frisch, Max, *Homo Faber*, 1957.
2 UNESCO, *Public library manifesto*, The Hague, IFLA, 1995.
3 DG XIII, *Fourth framework programme, call for proposals: libraries*, Brussels, European Commission, 1993.
4 Information Society 2000, *A Danish strategy for the information society*, 1996. **http://www.fsk.dk/fsk/pub/info2000-uk/**
5 Chancellor of the Duchy of Lancaster, *Government.direct, A prospectus for the electronic delivery of government services*, Cm 3438, London, HMSO, November 1996.
6 CCTA, *Report on information superhighways*, 1996. **http://www.open.gov.uk/ccta/reportv3.htm**
7 House of Lords, 5th Report of the Select Committee on Science and Technology, *Information society: agenda for action in the UK*, HL Paper 77, HMSO, 1996. **http://www.hmso.gov.uk/hmso/document/inforsoc.htm**
8 Department of National Heritage, *Reading the future, a review of public libraries in England*, March 1997.
9 Christchurch City Council, *Best IT practices in local government*, 1996, **http://xp8.dejanews.com/getdoc.xp?...&CONTEXT=850135242.12984&hitnum=49**
10 Gallimore, A., 'Putting partnership on the web', *Library Association record*, April 1996, 205.
11 British Library, *The information systems strategy*, 1995. **http://portico.bl.uk/iss/**
12 Higher Education Funding Council for England, *Joint Funding Council's Libraries Funding Review Group: report*, HEFCE, Bristol, 1993. **http://ukoln.bath.ac.uk/follett/follett_report.html**
13 MacColl, J., 'Information strategies get down to business', *Ariadne*, November 1996.
14 Coopers and Lybrand and the Joint Information Systems Committee's Information Strategies Steering Group,

Guidelines for developing an information strategy, Bristol, 1995.
http://www.niss.ac.uk/education/jisc/pub/infstrat/

15 Benton Foundation, *Buildings, books and bytes: libraries and communities in the digital age*, 1996.
http://www.benton.org/Kellogg/

16 Manchester City Council Arts and Leisure Committee, *IT strategy statement*, November 1995.

2 Benefits of an IT strategy

An integrated set of actions aimed at increasing the long-term well-being and strength of the enterprise relative to its competitors.

Definition of strategy: Ward[1]

Objectives
- ☐ **Define strategy**
- ☐ **Show the problems of a lack of strategy**
- ☐ **Indicate the benefits of a strategy.**

Strategy
Definition

'Strategy' is derived from a Greek word for taking charge of an army. The modern definition usually refers to generalship, including the art of deploying such resources as weapons and troops so as to dictate the turn of events in warfare. The fact that it has become a term used and probably abused by management theorists and consultants, who often see business as a battleground, should not deter its use in the relatively more peaceful context of IT developments. Most commercial organizations devise strategies to give themselves a competitive advantage over their rivals. In this sense they are following on from the military tradition of warriors gaining an advantage over their enemies by restricting their ability to engage.

The important analogy to be considered is the use of strategic planning to marshal the resources of the organization for maximum effectiveness in meeting future objectives. IT systems are expensive to implement and maintain, they require a change in the way an organization including a library service operates and they impose a new culture on the organization. For these reasons a well thought out strategy is essential.

Integration

An IT strategy should be integrated with the overall strategy or plans of the library service. It cannot exist as a separate entity with no reference to other developments. Many commercial organizations have seen the need to restructure themselves around an IT backbone that has become essential for their future success and survival. In these cases the management strategy of the company was identical to the IT strategy. The Institute of Chartered Accountants in England and Wales (ICAEW) has stressed the need for IT strategy to be integrated with the business planning process.[2] Libraries are also developing IT networks that form the backbone of their operations.

In practice, a good deal of IT development is often bottom-up, piecemeal and technology-driven rather than being integrated into the overall aims of the organization. Most organizations have experienced the system introduced by the amateur enthusiast for his or her own benefit, rather than the overall benefit of the organization, which remains the domain of the individual from which others are excluded. IT is only one component of the overall organizational strategy and must be integrated within that strategy. And IT must be owned by the whole of the management, not just by one or two enthusiasts.

An IT strategy should be more than just an outline of future intentions. It should also serve as a working plan for building a comprehensive range of IT facilities in the library service. An IT strategy can serve to improve the integration of an organization, particularly with the development of a shared network. It can be used to harness the efforts of different divisions of the organization.

A strategy does not spring fully formed from a few discussions by like-minded managers. In many organizations a strategy is often the unexpected end result of much searching and experimenting for solutions to what may be seen as intractable problems. A more logical approach to building a strategy is required.

The need for strategy
Problems of having no strategy

Without an IT strategy there is a danger that some of the benefits of localized applications may actually work against the overall aims of the library service and become counter-productive. Poor planning may leave systems with a shorter than expected lifespan and money may be spent developing systems more often than is necessary. Without a strategy the evolving needs of the library service may not be understood or dealt with.

There are risks in not having a strategy that blends in with the strategic movement of society itself. Opportunities may be missed if a library service diverges from its peers. There is a danger of fragmentation with libraries going their own ways with incompatible objectives. There is a danger of ignoring general trends which are expressed as expectations among users, whose needs must be to some extent anticipated. IT systems are expensive and must be part of a properly planned strategy if they are to achieve their purpose. Without a strategy there is the danger of unnecessary duplication of effort, either within the library service or between peers that ought to be cooperating. There is the risk of introducing systems in an *ad hoc* way which later turn out to be inflexible and incompatible with other systems, thus limiting their sphere of action. Systems may also turn out to be inefficient in their use of resources and produce imbalances of effort in the service.

Lost opportunities

Lack of a coherent strategy can lead to lost opportunities. A library may be placed at a disadvantage if it cannot interact with the IT developments of other organizations such as its suppliers. Older systems and technology investments which do not support the library's objectives can be a constraint to development. Poor integration or a lack of integration of systems may lead to poor data management which in turn can cause duplication of effort within the library service, inaccuracy, delays and inadequate information for management decision making. Priorities may become tied to the capabilities of inadequate systems rather than organizational objectives. Resources can be wasted on tasks that are devoted to maintaining ineffective and inefficient systems. If performance is held back because of inadequate systems, costs will be higher than they need be, productivity will be lower, and service will be poorer.

Divergence of aims

If IT planning is incoherent there will be a greater and greater divergence of aims, with incompatible systems being selected by different parts of an organization. Bringing diverse systems under control becomes an expensive process and often means replacing systems completely because they have limited connectibility. A lack of understanding between users, management and IT specialists can lead to conflict, poor solutions and a waste of resources. Without a strategy opportunism dictates how systems develop, often as pet projects by experts pursuing their own agendas. Initiatives are uncoordinated and uncontrolled and imbalances can develop, with resources being diverted to projects that are often peripheral to the main aims of the organization. Resources may thus become misused or wasted.

Proactive or reactive?

There is a need for libraries and information services to be more proactive in their approach to change. A strategy is a plan of action that is intended to drive the library service forward. In some cases the strategy will put the library service ahead of the expectations of its own users, anticipating their needs rather than reacting to demands late in the day when everyone else has already moved on. Libraries should not be afraid to be proactive in introducing new services and testing out new IT systems. There is a need to demonstrate that libraries can be at the cutting edge of developments in IT as well as other organizations.

Benefits
Benefits of producing a strategy

A strategy is not just a document or a set of ideas. It should be a plan of action which leads the library service forward in the pursuit of its objectives. The production of an IT strategy is a recognition that information and the technology to use information effectively now forms the backbone of many library and information services.

There are many benefits to be derived from the production of a coherent IT strategy itself, even before the strategy is implemented. Work on the strategy will draw attention to the importance the library puts on IT and will place IT developments at the top of the agenda. If the library has never produced a strategy before, the production of an IT strategy will mark a new departure for management and may stimulate debate about the need for a strategic approach in other areas.

The production of a concise strategy statement which can be circulated to staff, users, the governing body and outsiders can be an effective means for promoting the library's image and demonstrating the credibility of management.

Benefits of producing an IT strategy include:

☐ a clear sense of direction
☐ improved management credibility
☐ greater staff awareness and a shared responsibility for IT development
☐ more effective budget negotiations
☐ improved ability to bid for external funding
☐ an enhanced corporate image
☐ a more realistic view of the true capabilities of IT systems
☐ improved technical knowledge of IT.

The most important benefit of a well-formulated strategy is the clear sense of direction it provides for the library service.

In Manchester Public Libraries the IT strategy was used soon after it was produced to bid for capital funding.[3] The resulting capital provided was the largest amount the library service had ever received. IT was placed firmly at the top of the agenda for library developments for the next few years and there has been a significant increase in knowledge of IT systems by managers and other staff.

IT can be used to make fundamental changes in the structure of a library service that has become outmoded and behind the times. Radical rather than incremental change is often essential to success.

Benefits of implementing a strategy

There are further benefits that derive from the implementation of an IT strategy. These benefits relate to service delivery and operational management. With more efficient systems which are faster and easier to operate the quality of service to users should improve. New services which were not possible before can be provided, such as networked information services.

There is scope for increased income generation from some services. In Manchester Public Library, Internet access is charged for by the hour. In practice this is meant to cover the increased cost to the library of telephone charges but there is the potential to generate extra income from the service. Printouts from CD-ROM searching on the network generate income, with each sheet charged at 20p.

Benefits of implementation include:

☐ improved quality
☐ better communications
☐ improved management information and decision making
☐ improved and extended services for library users
☐ greater control and standardization
☐ risk reduction
☐ improved cost benefits
☐ greater efficiency
☐ increased income.

Incidental benefits

One of the benefits of the strategy process should be an increased awareness among the strategy team of IT systems and applications. There will be an increase in knowledge and skills developed during the course of the work which will be of benefit to the library service in future. The enthusiasm and commitment of senior management should be increased by the adoption of a formal strategy with such a fundamental role to play in the future of the library service. All staff who are made aware of the strategy can feel that the library service is moving with the times and will welcome the opportunity to learn new skills that will be of benefit to their future careers.

References

1   Ward, John and Griffiths, Pat, *Strategic planning for information systems*, 2nd edn, Wiley, Chichester, 1996, 63.
2   Institute of Chartered Accountants in England and Wales,

Developing your IT strategy – an integral part of business planning, 1996.
http://www.icaew.co.uk/depts/td/tditf/7td005.htm
3   Manchester City Council Arts and Leisure Committee, *IT strategy statement*, November 1995.

3 An outline of the IT strategy development process

The beginning is the most important part of the work.

Plato[1]

Objectives

☐ Outline the process for developing an IT strategy
☐ List the components of the process
☐ Illustrate the need for continuous strategy revision
☐ Indicate the problems in developing a strategy.

Strategy models
Different models

A number of models for the strategy process can be found in the literature on management, computing and information. These tend to be divided between those for IT strategies, IS strategies and information strategies. Reference has already been made in Chapter 1 to the Coopers and Lybrand report on the development of an information strategy.[2] There are many books and articles which relate to IS strategy in commercial organizations. Brown, for example describes the way businesses are developing strategies to integrate IT functions across their organizations in order to gain competitive advantage.[3] Ward hedges his bets by referring to IS/IT strategies but is nevertheless concerned to place IT strategy in the context of an overall business strategy.[4]

The different strategy models have many elements in common even though these may not be described in the same words. There are proponents for all three models, with legitimate claims for each. The process outlined here and expanded in detail in later chapters contains some elements in common with these models.

The main objective of an IT strategy, according to the ICAEW is '...to provide a framework for the development, acquisition, and use of IT in furtherance of agreed business plans and objectives'.[5] This applies equally in a library service to any other organization. The process outlined below will provide such a framework.

Simplifying the process

The terminology of IT seems almost a separate language and may present difficulties to the uninitiated. Some technical and management terminology is unavoidable but an attempt has been made to minimize the jargon. The process has been simplified as much as possible. Complicated diagrams and artificial labels have been avoided in favour of a straightforward explanation of the components of the process.

A strategy can eventually be abbreviated to a strategy statement, a useful document for communicating the broad intentions, but the strategy itself is not simply a document. It is a process. The purpose of an IT strategy is to map out a process that can be followed from beginning to end in order to move the library service forward to a position of advantage.

The strategy development process
Components of the process

The strategy development process can be clarified by considering the component parts individually. A project plan for the process, divided into stages with a list of tasks and timescales for completing them, should be drawn up.

The essential components of the strategy development process are:

☐ the aims
☐ the scope
☐ internal audit
☐ external environment
☐ physical infrastructure building blocks
☐ policy and management considerations
☐ evaluation of the IT strategy
☐ implementation plans

☐ monitoring and review.

These are explained in more detail below.

The aims

At the beginning of the strategy development process the aims should be outlined clearly with objectives to be achieved. Senior management support must be obtained and resources for developing the strategy allocated. It is essential that adequate time and effort is spent on the process and resources are assigned to it.

The scope

The starting point for developing the strategy is to establish the ground rules. These include the scope or coverage of the strategy and the terms of reference, how the strategy is to be approached and the people involved in producing it. The roles of the different people involved and their different levels of responsibilities must be defined.

Internal audit

The internal environment of the library service must be examined in detail. This will include a review of existing management strategy and plans, and an examination of the needs of users and the needs of the library service as a whole. An audit of existing IT facilities is needed to establish the basis for change or further development. Some libraries may already have an existing infrastructure which may be a dominant influence on the development of the strategy.

External environment

The external environment in which the library service operates must be examined for any threats and opportunities. This will include any external influences on the library service which may have an impact on IT. An obvious example is the budget decisions of the funding body.

The examples of libraries and other organizations in introducing innovative IT projects should be assessed for potential applications. The aim of this research is to develop a strategic overview of what IT systems are available in the IT marketplace and to develop enough knowledge of its potential to make sound decisions on whether it can be used effectively in the library.

Physical infrastructure building blocks

Once enough information has been gathered from the research, the main body of the strategy can be constructed as a series of building blocks. These will form the proposals for future IT developments. The building blocks will consist of the physical elements of the IT infrastructure such as networks, hardware and software.

Policy and management considerations

Accompanying the physical elements of the IT strategy should be policies surrounding the use of IT and the management processes needed to operate IT systems and services effectively. Policies may cover such things as auditing, security, contingency plans, upgrading and replacement procedures. Management processes include such things as the planning of facilities, network management, supplier management, the provision of technical support to users, training considerations, staffing and management of IT services. Details of organizational changes which may be necessary as a result of the introduction of new IT systems should also be included.

Evaluation of the IT strategy

Once the basic outline of the strategy has been developed the implications must be evaluated against a number of criteria prior to full implementation. Senior management must be satisfied that the strategy is feasible and that the resources can be found to implement it. Assurances will be sought that the skills needed for implementation either exist within the library service or can be obtained when needed. The obstacles to implementation must be identified and plans formulated to deal with them. The most important and intransigent of these may be the prevailing culture of the library service. Where alternative solutions have been proposed the best option must be chosen, bearing in mind the risks involved in moving forward as opposed to doing nothing. Some estimate of the benefits to be obtained compared with the costs involved must be produced so that IT developments can be justified against other demands upon increasingly restricted budgets. Once a strategy has been approved it is divided into a number of projects and the main management concern is then one of control over the implementation of the strategy.

Implementation plans

When approval has been obtained for the strategy, more detailed plans for implementation should be drawn up. These will consist of a number of separate projects which have been costed and prioritized by senior management. The consequences of implementation need to be carefully assessed. If funding is obtained for the implementation plan then implementation proper can be undertaken. The process will include the production of specifications and possibly offers to tender.

Monitoring

The main reason for monitoring is to measure the effectiveness of the implementation programme. Monitoring should indicate where there are problems in the implementation or in the acceptance of new systems within the library service. The monitoring will be a mixture of quantitative and qualitative measures. Statistics can be derived from the systems to indicate precisely what use is being made of the new facilities. CD-ROMs on a network, for example, can be monitored accurately, with the use of each title and of each terminal or password automatically logged for detailed analysis.

In addition to the collection of usage statistics, it is important to gather information about the reaction of users to the new systems. This may be done by questionnaire if there are many users in an organization and by the use of sample interviews. User groups may be established to give feedback at regular meetings on problems and to share ideas. If feasible, the establishment of an internal bulletin board on a network could be useful in identifying problems and difficulties with new systems by monitoring the messages.

As well as internal monitoring, the external environment must continue to be monitored. The purpose of external monitoring is to ensure that the implementation programme is not undermined by external changes. Rapid changes in hardware and software can render systems obsolete within a couple of years unless sufficient flexibility is built into the process. Changes in political or economic circumstances can also affect the long-term implementation programme, for example if there is a change in expected expenditure because of a budget increase or decrease.

Review

Any concerns identified in the monitoring process need to be fed through to the strategy itself. The strategy should be capable of being altered to take account of changed circumstances. If this is not done there is a danger that the strategy may begin to move off on a tangent away from the mainstream of IT developments. The library service may then find itself hampered with systems that few others are using. This may prevent the library service from making effective links with others in the future. Other problems might include difficulty in finding staff with the necessary knowledge to run the system, difficulty in getting support for hardware, software etc. Systems developed in-house are particularly prone to this problem.

Using the strategy development process
The sequence

The components of the strategy process outlined above can be used as a series of steps in developing an IT strategy for the library or information service, although it is unlikely that they will be used in a strictly chronological order. Some of the research work could be done in parallel, especially if tasks are divided between members of a team. Each component of the process is explained in more detail in a later chapter, with guidance on how it should be dealt with. The chapters have been arranged as a sequence of activities for the development of a complete IT strategy.

Different needs

The process does not seek to impose the same IT strategy upon every library, it is merely a path to follow to develop a strategy that will meet the specific needs of an individual library or information service. There will be differences in the application of the strategy process in different library services. One of the factors influencing the process will be the size of the library service: a large library service will have more resources to devote to the strategy process but will also have more complex problems to deal with; a small library service with fewer resources to allocate to the process may find the work difficult to justify to the same level of detail. Even so, it should be possible to identify the more important points of the process and concentrate on those which are a priority.

Success factors

The success of the strategy development process will depend partly upon the starting point of the exercise, including how useful the existing systems are. It will also depend on the opportunities for future applications and picking out likely winning project ideas which will have a big impact on the library service. It will also depend on the extent to which senior management is involved and seen to be giving full backing to the strategy development as a management priority.

Continuous strategy development

Dealing with IT is similar to clay pigeon shooting: the target is always moving, one needs to aim slightly ahead of the target in order to score a successful hit, environmental factors can easily obscure the view of the target and even when the target has been hit the recoil may have unexpected consequences.

Developing a strategy is not a one-off exercise but rather part of an evolutionary process. The IT strategy must be regularly revised and improved as objectives are achieved and the benefits from one cycle are fed into the next. New options and opportunities will arise from outside the library service and within it. IT itself is always changing and the changes must be constantly monitored for new opportunities. The library service itself will change significantly as it moves forward towards new levels of service and provision.

Outputs

Initially documents will be the main physical outputs of the strategy process. These should provide an overview of the current situation and a blueprint for the future development of the library service, with plans for specific achievements and milestones for assessing progress. An abbreviated strategy statement should be published to inform staff and interested parties of the library service's intentions. There will be reports to the steering group, management team or funding body at intervals. In this case, charts, diagrams and any other outputs should be kept to a minimum and should be as simple as possible. More detailed models, including computer-based project schedules may be required later depending upon the complexity of the organization and the range of its plans.

Problems in developing a strategy
Commitment and resources

There are a number of problems which can prevent a strategy being developed effectively. There may be difficulty in obtaining commitment from senior management to implement the strategy. Senior management may not find the time needed for input into the strategy. There may be difficulty in finding the right person to manage the production of the strategy. Funding for the work in producing the strategy may not be forthcoming. There may be difficulty in finding the right mix of people to help in the processes of preparing the strategy. If existing relationships between system users and IT personnel are distant or problematic this may prevent an objective strategy being formulated.

To produce an effective strategy it is essential that experienced, skilled and well-motivated people are involved who are committed to the process and prepared to invest the time needed to do the work properly. More details of the skills needed for the process are given in Chapter 4.

The learning process

Developing a strategy is a learning process for the participants and for the whole library service. Library services which have not yet developed a strategy may not know how to go about it. There is a big difference between reacting to the short-term demands for IT systems from knowledgeable individuals or the ever-increasing wish lists produced at the hint of incidental funding and the far-from-easy task of planning for the present and future needs of the whole library service. Timescales for a strategy including implementation of the priority elements are likely to be two to three years. Development should be carried forward by future priorities rather than incremental changes to existing systems. There may need to be a gradual progress through a list designed to satisfy the various political factions and alliances that vie for resources in an organization.

At the end of the day, an organization will get the systems it deserves.

References

1   Plato, *The Republic*, Bk 1, 377 – B.
2   Coopers and Lybrand and the Joint Information Systems Committee's Information Strategies Steering Group, *Guidelines for developing an information strategy*, Bristol, 1995.
    http://www.niss.ac.uk/education/jisc/pub/infstrat/
3   Brown, A., 'Getting value from an integrated IS strategy', *European journal of information systems*, April 1994, 155–65.
4   Ward, John and Griffiths, Pat, *Strategic planning for information systems*, 2nd edn, Wiley, Chichester, 1996.
5   Institute of Chartered Accountants in England and Wales, *Developing your IT strategy – an integral part of business planning*, 1996.
    http://www.icaew.co.uk/depts/td/tditf/7td005.htm

4 Aims and scope of the strategy

In everything one must consider the end.

Jean de La Fontaine[1]

Objectives

- Establish the aims of the strategy
- Obtain senior management support
- Set up a steering group
- Define the limits of the strategy
- Set up a strategy team
- Obtain the resources to carry out the work.

Establishing the aims of the strategy
Initial questions

There are a number of preliminary questions which need to be asked about the strategy process before any aims are defined:

- What is the main purpose or the driving force for the development of the strategy?
- What problems and constraints are likely to affect the outcome of the process?
- What are the expectations and objectives to meet in developing the strategy?
- How can full support be obtained from other people in the organization who need to be consulted or involved in the formulation of the strategy?
- What techniques will be employed in developing the strategy?
- What resources are available for the process?
- What is the timescale for producing the strategy?

☐ How should the process be managed?
☐ What will the exercise cost?

The larger and more complex the library or information service the more work will be needed and the more costly the exercise will be. If there is a tight deadline to meet then research may have to be limited and objectives scaled down. Negotiating for adequate time and resources will be necessary if the process is to be carried out properly.

Driving forces

☐ The main driving force may be the need to consider IT as part of the overall service plan or the regular cycle of organizational objectives.
☐ Legislation may be the driving force, such as the need for some public libraries to introduce radical change and major restructuring after the move towards unitary local authorities.
☐ The funding body may be the main catalyst for change, for example in the need to rationalize resources after budget reductions, which are becoming more and more common in public institutions.
☐ There may be new opportunities opened up by mergers between departments or institutions.
☐ Peer pressure may force changes where the library service would be at a disadvantage compared to other similar institutions which compete for its customers or users of its services.
☐ Users may themselves be the main force for change by demanding such new facilities as open learning or distance learning.
☐ Suppliers may create pressure to adapt if their own systems are becoming more dependent upon IT.

Setting objectives for the strategy

The first task in any planning process is to set objectives. Defining the aims of the strategy provides the broad framework of principles on which the detailed IT systems planning can be built. The objectives may include:

Needs
- ☐ Identifying current and future information needs.
- ☐ Developing policies for the creation, maintenance and control of organizational information resources.
- ☐ Creating a dependable IT infrastructure in order to deliver quality information services.
- ☐ Looking at the future growth of the library service and its functions and how needs will change.

Services
- ☐ Introducing new services which were not possible before.
- ☐ Improving the value of services offered to users.
- ☐ Providing equal access to information for all users by making facilities available throughout the library service and eventually extending access to users at remote sites, including home access.
- ☐ Improving the flexibility of existing systems to cater for the creative use of IT by users.

Management
- ☐ Ensuring that IT is brought to the top of the organization's agenda.
- ☐ Ensuring representation for IT at senior management level.
- ☐ Mapping out an effective organizational structure for the IT function.
- ☐ Ensuring that the IT strategy is widely communicated throughout the organization.

Flexibility
- ☐ Making sure the IT function is flexible enough to be able to respond to changing needs.
- ☐ Creating an open systems policy and adopting open standards and protocols which will enable the library service to link into external systems.
- ☐ Ensuring the smooth integration of new and existing systems.

Staff skills
- ☐ Identifying the necessary staff skills for the effective utilization of IT in the library service.
- ☐ Incorporating within the staff structure posts dedicated to managing and maintaining IT systems and creating new services

from them.
☐ Improving the efficiency of staff by training and making the most effective use of organizational information systems.

Partnerships
☐ Developing cooperative schemes and partnerships with other organizations locally, regionally or nationally for the joint development of IT projects, including those which will benefit the local community.

Commercially oriented organizations will be concerned also with improving profits or income generation, increasing market share, growing the market or entering new markets, developing new products and services, expanding abroad etc.

Overview of the organization

An overview of the organization needs to be obtained by looking at its long-term goals, its vision for the future, its general strategy as an organization, what the main forces for change are, what initiatives are planned for change, its present structure, values, culture, management style and performance. All of these may have an impact upon the IT strategy.

Mission statement

The organizational objectives should reflect the values of the organization, the management, the users and the funding or governing body. Many organizations express these values in the form of a succinct mission statement. The mission statement concerns the purpose of the organization and its long-term aims and is not intended to be measured in quantifiable terms. Such a statement is intended to be in use for many years to come. The IT strategy should incorporate the same values as the mission statement. In many large organizations IT has become such an important part of their operations that the mission statement itself includes references to IT.

Organizational objectives

The major objectives of the library service will change from year to year, evolving in line with changes both within and outside the organization. A more detailed examination of the library service's annual service plans or objectives should be undertaken to see if there is any likely conflict with the aims of the IT strategy or if they contain any opportunities for potential IT applications.

Senior management support

Support from senior management is vital for the successful implementation of any strategy, although it may be difficult to obtain in some organizations. Senior managers may lack awareness of the impact of IT generally and may not see the long-term advantages. Some may be used to seeing IT in terms of specific operational systems, such as issuing systems in libraries, rather than strategic systems which are having a fundamental influence on society and its institutions. They may feel there is a great deal of hype surrounding IT and are cynical about the benefits it offers. Internally, managers tend to give low priority to establishing effective management information systems and only appreciate the need when they require facts urgently.

These attitudes have begun to change with the realization that computers are more than just a technical problem for experts to deal with. Senior managers need to know more about the strategic impact of IT and to be more closely involved in IT developments. IT affects many strategic decisions because it is at the core of many services. Many organizations could not function without IT systems, being effectively locked in by the needs of their users, their suppliers and the need for efficient internal operations which depend upon electronic information. The fact that IT has become so complex, cutting across traditional organizational boundaries and functions, means that senior management must be involved in major decisions about the use of IT.

IT accounts for a large and increasing expenditure. In many organizations IT regularly accounts for between 5% and 10% of revenue and up to 50% of all capital expenditure. Return on investment is important to senior managers who have many conflicting priorities and not enough resources to deal with them all. For this reason alone, senior managers should be capable of understanding IT sufficiently well to make sound judgements about new investments.

The benefits of IT are rarely seen in cost savings but more often in terms of improved services, as has been shown above. However, recent trends in the public sector have been to cut costs to deal with falling budgets rather than to improve services which already meet the perceived low expectations of users. With continual cutbacks and falling budgets in public services there has been a tendency in recent years to concentrate on short-term aims and crisis management rather than longer-term strategic management.

IT must be near the top of the senior management agenda and managers must be able to evaluate IT systems with confidence and authority rather than leaving the decisions to technical experts and advisers.

Without senior management support an IT strategy is no more than a paper exercise.

Steering groups

Most organizations developing a strategy will form a steering group to oversee the process. This will be a group of senior people in the organization who are best able to judge the performance of a strategy development team and who can determine whether the IT strategy is developing along the lines of the organization's overall management strategy. These might include senior staff with IT knowledge, financial management skills, staff development skills or who have responsibility for major areas affected by IT. In this case, a member of the senior management team should act as leader or coordinator.

The senior management team may be the best forum for steering the process. In some organizations a steering group may be formed solely for the purpose, chaired by someone at a senior level. The role of the group would be to:

☐ oversee the development of the strategy, including providing resources for the process
☐ approve the IT strategy once it has been formulated and documented
☐ decide on priority projects for implementation
☐ agree the resources needed for implementation
☐ monitor progress towards the objectives of the strategy
☐ communicate its intentions across the organization to develop support for the strategy

Defining the scope of the strategy
Long-term plans

The scope must be defined early on so that the strategy team or the individual given the task of producing the strategy is clear about what is expected. A strategy is meant to provide a long-term view for the library service and would normally cover developments for the next three to five years. This means that the scope can be quite wide and will encompass all the main operations of the library service. The scope may extend to include an examination of all information processes in the library or the wider organization with a view to computerising all shared information. On the other hand, it might be unrealistic to try to cover all needs in detail in one step.

Constraints

There may be constraints applied to the scope of the strategy such as:

☐ excluding recommendations on specific hardware and software
☐ leaving out remote sites of the organization and concentrating on a central location
☐ concentrating on services to users
☐ leaving internal management information needs to a later date
☐ working within a restricted budget
☐ looking at developments on a shorter timescale.

Restricting the scope too much would result in an incomplete solution which by its nature could not be called a strategy. The scope could be revisited and redefined later after more work has been done on establishing the context in which the strategy is being developed. In fact, it is likely that boundaries will change as research uncovers more information about the needs of the service or about the opportunities for IT developments. This should not be an excuse to continue gathering information indefinitely and a deadline should be set for completing the work on the strategy.

Carrying out the work

The strategy team

Mention has already been made of a strategy team which will do the work in putting together the strategy. The size of this team depends on the size of the organization and on the size of the task it faces. There are few, if any, libraries which do not have some sort of computer system, though some older systems may be reaching the end of their useful life and need to be replaced. One individual may be all that is required in some libraries, with additional support from other staff. However many people are required, it is essential that they are given adequate time for the work to be carried out.

Some training may be needed at this stage in project planning. It is common in some organizations for project definition workshops to be held in which the aims of the project are thoroughly worked out with the team members so that each one understands clearly the role that he or she has to play in the process.

The work might be contracted out to an outside organization or consultancy. This might prove to be expensive and, in the case of a consultancy, the tendency is for standard methodologies to be used which might not be wholly appropriate for the library service. No one is likely to understand the internal nuances and politics of a library service as well as the staff who work in it and for this reason it is better to use internal staff for the work.

The skills needed for the work include:

- ☐ project planning
- ☐ time management
- ☐ research and information gathering
- ☐ computer knowledge
- ☐ management knowledge
- ☐ general knowledge of library activities.

The strategy manager

The strategy must be effectively managed to ensure that its objectives match and support those of the organization, and that potential opportunities are identified and exploited. An important factor in the successful outcome of any IT strategy will be the person responsible for managing the strategy process by leading the strategy team. This person must be able to understand the reason why each part of the strategy process is necessary and be capable of carrying it forward. A clear understanding of the strategy process is needed. The ability to overcome obstacles to the process and to sell the results to senior management and other staff in the library service is essential.

The strategy manager must be capable of:

☐ developing an unbiased overview of the library service and its problems
☐ maintaining a consistent approach to the different parts of the strategy
☐ producing consistent documented outputs
☐ communicating effectively between the strategy team and the rest of the library service
☐ breaking down the strategy into a series of comprehensible units
☐ making decisions on the priorities to be assigned to the most important elements

The emphasis should be on providing practical options that can be delivered. The IT culture proposed should match the overall culture of the library service. Achieving the best balance between centralized and decentralized control is also one of the main aims.

Obtaining resources to carry out the work

The objectives, scope and expected outcomes should be confirmed with senior management. Any resources needed for the research should be obtained, e.g. computer resources. Information gathering will be necessary and much of this is likely to be technical. Interviews may need to be undertaken with appropriate staff in the library service who are responsible for different aspects of IT. Other staff may also need to be consulted if their work has potential for computerization. Those already using IT systems that may in future be integrated will need to be consulted. Clearly identifying with the existing problems in the organization will ensure that the strategy is developed in line with the needs of management. There is obviously a cost involved in developing a strategy and there must be a convincing justification for the work undertaken.

Part of the resulting strategy must be to show that the cost was justified and will be offset by future benefits.

References

1   La Fontaine, Jean de, *Fables*, Bk 3, Fable 5.

5 Internal audit

Organisations gather information and don't use it. They ask for more information and then ignore it. They make decisions first and look for the relevant information afterward. In fact, organisations seem to gather a great deal of information that has little or no decision-making relevance.

March[1]

Objectives
- [ ] Obtain an overview of the overall management strategy
- [ ] Include plans for information management
- [ ] Assess user and organizational needs
- [ ] Undertake an IT audit
- [ ] Assess human assets for IT development
- [ ] Assess physical assets and liabilities of buildings etc.

Existing organizational strategy
Strategic plans

An IT strategy must be designed to integrate with the overall management strategy of the library and the parent organization. Most organizations produce service plans, annual budgets and a variety of other plans for the year ahead. Some have plans for several years ahead, often as part of wider corporate initiatives. Such plans, whether documented or existing only in the minds of senior management, must be taken into account in the IT strategy to ensure that there is no possibility of conflict between them. IT systems will have an impact upon broader strategic plans. They may make possible what had been only a hope or an idea. The impact may be sufficiently great to cause a major change of direction in policy.

The main questions to be considered include:

- [ ] Is there a strategic plan for the next few years?

☐ What are the library service's main areas for future development?

☐ What is the present management structure and how are decisions made?

☐ Do other separate strategies exist, e.g. for future finances, staff resources or services to users?

In smaller libraries or where a senior manager is leading the strategy team such information may already be well known and the process may be considerably shortened. If no plans exist, there will be a need to spend more time in researching the views of senior staff about future policies.

Gathering views

There may be a need for interviews with senior staff, workshops with a representative selection of staff throughout the library service, or brainstorming sessions to gather a wide range of views. The intention is to establish an overview of the direction the library service intends to take in the future and how IT can be incorporated into this. Such research is also useful for spreading the idea about the strategy and building support for it.

The work may identify areas where policies are not yet properly formulated or where change is occurring which might have consequences for the scope of the strategy as it was originally defined. There may be issues which will have to be excluded because they too are uncertain. Other issues that are just beginning to emerge may need to be taken into account because they may quickly assume a greater importance. Recent changes in the Net Book Agreement (NBA) and Copyright Regulations, for example, have had an impact upon many library services. New relationships have been negotiated between libraries and suppliers as a result of the abandonment of the NBA which have acted as a spur to the introduction of electronic approval systems and ordering and investigations into the use of Electronic Data Interchange (EDI).

Organizational culture

An understanding of the current position of the library service and how it operates is needed if the IT strategy is to be relevant to its needs. The existing culture of the library service is an important factor in the success or failure of any new system, whether IT-based or not. The culture of the library service, including its staffing structure, the relationships existing within it, the attitudes of staff, and the ability of management to introduce effective new processes, must be assessed. The library service's ability to adapt to change must be accurately determined.

Strengths and weaknesses

Understanding the current position and purpose of the organization internally can be done by examining its strengths and weaknesses, the opportunities and threats to its services. This SWOT analysis is a well-known tool employed in marketing and general business and organizational planning. Although it is not intended to offer any solutions to problems it is useful in obtaining a clear picture of the present situation. This requires an analysis of the resources available in the library including the range of services offered to users.

Information strategy
The importance of information

The importance of information in information technology must be stressed. The technology is secondary to the information. Information permeates all organizations; it must be considered part of the infrastructure. Information includes text, data, images and sounds whether in electronic form or not. It is worth considering information as a separate thread in the strategy process.

Information is important at an operational level, at the administration or control level and at the strategic management level. Information is at the centre of any organization and provides the means by which knowledge is acquired by the people in that organization, enabling them to work more effectively with a clear understanding of their roles and objectives.

Successful handling of information is central to the success and effectiveness of the organization. Systems for making the most effective use of information are needed at all levels and these should be integrated so that information can flow from one level to another without restraint. Unfortunately, in many organizations there will be a legacy of different systems at different levels which cannot communicate with each other and which actually prevent the flow of information through the organization. A simple illustration of this is the standalone word-processing system preferred by one staff member which uses a different software package from everyone else, the files of which are not available, the information on which is inaccessible. Much time can be wasted trying to convert a document from one format to another.

The larger the organization the more fragmented the information is likely to be. Although a large proportion of the information may be computerized it is likely that only a small fraction is effectively managed.

Benefits of information management

Many organizations are realizing the advantages of having information management policies. Managing and exploiting the information generated within organizations can produce increased benefits in the form of efficiency savings, increased management productivity and effectiveness. Providing accessible information allows an organization to respond quickly and with more confidence to changes in direction, changing user needs, changes in funding or policy changes provoked by external agents.

Sharing information can help to improve communication between staff, resolve areas of conflict, prevent duplication of effort and generate ideas. Cooperative working can lead to greater synergy in which the gains are greater than the individual contributions might otherwise have been. Opportunities are often lost when information is not communicated or cannot be obtained in time. Information may have a value beyond the organization in which it was created and could be used to generate income. Integrating the flow of information between individuals can provide better and speedier access to information when it is needed. Documents held on a central server and retrieved through desktop computers can save time and effort for managers preparing reports, for groups working on joint projects and for staff who need occasional access to procedures and technical manuals. The networking of information has become the major growth area in the use of computers in the last few years. Many organizations have realized the potential of providing almost immediate access to information for staff in an environment which is changing rapidly and requires equally rapid decision making.

Information management

The effective management of information resources within an organization requires a holistic approach. Information management, sometimes called by other names such as information resource management (IRM) or corporate data management, is a method of viewing information as a vital resource which can be used to add value to the organization. The objective is to achieve the integrated, efficient and economic management of all the information in the organization – getting the right information to the right people, in the right form, at the right time. An information audit of the organization may be necessary in order to develop a plan for the strategic management of information. This should not be undertaken lightly because it will involve a considerable amount of work and is likely to take several months to complete.

Information Management involves:

☐ listing sources and types of information in the organization
☐ identifying the organization's real information needs
☐ allocating responsibilities for information to staff and users
☐ establishing levels for different information users, e.g. raw data, aggregrated, summaries
☐ measuring the cost effectiveness of information provision
☐ designing appropriate preparation, storage and retrieval systems
☐ drawing up procedures and guidelines for data input, amendment and storage
☐ establishing standards for data quality, accuracy, security and timeliness
☐ ensuring compliance with the Data Protection Act
☐ cataloguing information resources for easier retrieval
☐ determining the scope for information sharing
☐ developing procedures and controls for authorizing access and maintaining security
☐ developing routines for housekeeping activities such as data backup and archiving
☐ planning for recovery after system failure
☐ drawing up procedures to monitor use of information
☐ providing appropriate systems for users to create, store, share, retrieve and use information
☐ making users aware of the information available and how it can be accessed

☐ promoting awareness of the benefits of information sharing.

A common trend nowadays is to provide all functions through a single desktop terminal with standalone facilities, access to internal network servers, often including an Intranet, and access via gateways on the network to external information resources including the Internet.

Information management should result in a set of policies and procedures for defining how information is to be generated and managed. It will also cover the acquisition of information, data protection and how information should be disseminated and used. The administration and maintenance of information resources, whether by a central authority such as the IT unit or by departments and individuals, should be defined. The services that operate to deliver information to users and the tools needed to access information should be stipulated. The procedures for sharing information should be documented and staff trained in the efficient use of systems and procedures.

In most organizations the task of trying to integrate all internal information would be too great to tackle in one process. The degree of management of existing information will be determined by priorities within the organization. Management will involve establishing procedures to ensure consistency, accuracy and reliability of information and standards to which users must conform in preparing and storing information. This is particularly important at the operational level of an organization where large databases are often the basis of service delivery. In a library this would be based upon the catalogue and the issue and discharge functions. Information management also applies higher up the organization's management hierarchy. At these levels the needs of individuals for creative freedom to use their own desktop facilities must be reconciled with the organization's need for standardization to allow information to be shared effectively and made accessible beyond the individual desktop.

The development of hypertext documents and the establishment of Intranets on which documents are effectively linked together and immediately retrievable is making information easier to share and more accessible. Fewer controls are needed to prepare and format documents and multimedia can be incorporated easily within the documents. However, the same rules will apply in terms of information management if information sharing and retrieval is to be effective.

Research for information management

Information flow through the organization can be mapped to create a picture of the present situation. This will give an indication of whether existing systems are capable of satisfying the organization's needs for information provision, whether they need to be enhanced or replaced. The current information that is generated, stored and archived should be examined to see whether it is needed and whether there are any gaps. A plan for more effective information flows can be drawn up which will indicate a gradual changeover from existing systems and procedures. The infrastructure needed to ensure effective flow of information will be designed as part of the overall IT strategy, identifying and utilizing as far as possible any existing information that can be transferred into a more consolidated and accessible base for sharing.

External information sources

The total information environment of an organization includes external information which the organization draws in from users, suppliers, competitors, peer organizations, government etc. The external environment is especially volatile and cannot be subjected to any effective control. The information can be difficult to obtain and often comes at a price, which can be a direct cost or an indirect cost in terms of the time taken to retrieve it. Online information retrieval, access to CD-ROMs on a network and the Internet are all now available through desktop terminals to provide people with the information they need. Information is needed to find out about new developments from suppliers, new products which might increase staff efficiency or improve services. The policies and developments of similar organizations should also be monitored for ideas. Access to newsgroups and listservers via e-mail is particularly useful for following debates on topical issues and reading the results of practical surveys on topics of mutual interest. External databases with statistical or market information can be useful. Online searches of the appropriate literature as part of preparatory research before embarking upon project work are essential. Information retrieval is essentially a one-way communication process but there is a need to communicate information to others as well as retrieve information from passive information stores.

External communication

Efficient communication with external suppliers, users, colleagues and others is a necessary factor in any information management strategy. This will include electronic communication through e-mail, the sending and receiving of electronic text and multimedia files and online software delivery. Librarians may want to search the catalogues of other libraries, to order books and other materials through interlibrary loan functions as well as to access remote data and documents. The provision of such facilities is part of the overall management of information in the organization.

Problems of information management

To provide effective access to information in an organization is not easy. Information often resides in many files created by a number of different software packages on a range of systems. The files can be poorly documented or organized and because they are stored on many standalone PCs are usually inaccessible to anyone but the person who created them. This legacy of uncontrolled development is made worse by the fact that some information will be inconsistent in format, poorly prepared, eccentric in presentation and varied in structure. Created by different people, at different times, for different reasons, using different standards and different terminology, much information is inconsistent and difficult to use even when it is accessible.

Information that is held centrally may have a better chance of being consistent and prepared to a standard. Central databases have usually had more controls exerted over input than word-processed documents, for example. Information is exchanged across organizations by a mixture of media including voice, printed materials, faxes, electronic messages and text. In most organizations there will be a large volume of uncomputerized and often unrecorded information making it to all intents and purposes inaccessible to those who may need it.

Information management strategy

An IT strategy must take into account the need for the effective management of information across the organization. Information needs must be prioritized so that they are based on the objectives of the organization rather than on the technology wish lists of individuals. Whether introducing IT for the first time or reorganizing existing systems, the aim should be to plan an integrated flow of information through the organization. Standards need to be applied to manage information effectively. These will include information preparation including adherence to standard report formats, standards for file formats and file naming, standards for file storage and some form of indexing for future retrieval.

The end result of the process should be the formulation of a set of policies and objectives for effective information management, a plan for the development of an information infrastructure, a detailed plan for organizational information for effective retrieval and a schedule for introducing information management across the organization.

Assessment of user and organizational needs
User needs and expectations

Library services are making more and more use of IT as part of their direct delivery of services to users and this trend will continue. The trend is towards end-user access to IT systems in libraries. There are pressures from all sections of society for libraries to increase their IT facilities. New IT-based media are appearing all the time. Multimedia and bibliographic CD-ROMs, shareware, Internet access, computer-based open learning etc. are all placing new demands upon resources.

A new generation of computer-literate students and school-children is no longer satisfied with using only print-based information. Trying to keep pace with all the new forms of delivery of electronic information and the capital and revenue investment needed is becoming increasingly problematic. Library users expect libraries to provide IT facilities in addition to the more traditional printed information media but the cost of doing so is often greater than resources permit. Understanding the needs of users is essential.

An internal audit could not be complete without looking at the needs of users. Users may be employees within the library service, users of the library's services or suppliers and collaborators who will need access to the internal systems of the library for effective interaction.

There may be pressure from employees who see themselves

falling behind colleagues elsewhere or who can see ways of improving their own work by the introduction of IT. These concerns must be taken into account although the expectations of some individuals may have to be ignored if these are too ambitious for the library service as a whole. Conversely, the expectations of others may have to be raised if an individual idea is worth applying throughout the organization. Few people appreciate the benefits of e-mail, for example, until they have been trained to use it, and thus have low expectations of its value.

Needs surveys

A survey of user needs may be necessary if little is known about them, for example if the library service is large and complex with many sites. It is likely that some users will have made their needs known in one way or another, probably in informal ways to management. This ad hoc evidence of need is insufficient except as a stimulus for further investigation. The aim of carrying out a survey is to obtain an unbiased and balanced view of needs and to allow as many people as possible to participate in the strategy process. Lovecy has stressed the importance of this work in gaining user support for the IT strategy.[2]

The survey should aim to determine from users:

☐ what systems they need
☐ how they use IT systems
☐ when and where they need access
☐ what they will use the systems for
☐ what advantages they would obtain from them
☐ the problems they may find in accessing and using them.

Where systems are already in use the aim may be to determine possible shortcomings or deficiencies and ideas users may have for improvements.

Reconciling different needs

Sometimes there may be problems in meeting the needs of different groups of users on one system. For example, different needs for security must be reconciled when the same database system is used by management for diagnostic purposes, operational staff for data creation and maintenance and external users for information retrieval.

Management needs vary from the retrieval of management information to the provision of effective communication facilities. The ready accessibility of internal information for decision making is one of the most vital concerns. The ability to manipulate data locally is also important.

Operational staff require systems that are easy to use, reliable and accurate. Transactions must be fast, secure and free of error.

Technical staff need systems that are easy to set up and maintain with automatic diagnostic facilities and the ability to deal with problems remotely.

Users want systems that meet a comprehensive range of information needs, can be learned quickly, work in an intuitive way and are available at the right times. Facilities for printing or downloading information are essential. Simple access procedures with few formalities are desirable.

Assessing the needs of users should highlight gaps in provision and improvements which need to be made to existing procedures.

Organizational needs

IT should be a solution to an organizational need. It should not be introduced for its own sake. If there is no urgent need for the production of publicity materials in-house then there is little justification for introducing a desktop publishing system with all the training and effort that would need to be invested in it.

Assessing user needs is important and can reveal a great deal of useful information but the needs of the organization itself must also be examined objectively. Users tend to express needs for solutions to current or personal problems. The library service should have a vision of its own future and where it expects to be in the years ahead. The intention should be to produce a series of policy statements about the future of the library service, the direction in which it is moving in or would like to move, the infrastructure it wishes to develop and the future management and organizational structure it needs to succeed. The statements should apply to the next three to five years.

A strategy should ensure as far as possible that both sets of needs are met while avoiding any conflict between them. Where there is conflict the needs of the library service must obviously take precedence over those of individuals. The earlier examination of the library service's strategy will have indicated the direction it wishes to move in and the position it expects to reach in the future. The purpose of the internal audit is to determine what IT systems could be introduced to support the library service in achieving its strategic goals.

IT audit
Purpose of the audit

An IT audit is an examination of the existing IT systems in the library or information service.

The main purposes of the IT audit are to identify gaps in provision and assess the potential for updating or extending existing systems to improve services to users. Some of the main considerations will be:

☐ The effectiveness of so-called legacy IT systems – those older systems which have been inherited and are still in use for particular functions – will need to be assessed.
☐ Current operational IT systems and applications and any planned for the near future will also need to be assessed.
☐ The existing position of IT in the library service must be understood including its scope, structure and the skills and experience which presently exist to support it.
☐ The financial situation of the library service is important including the construction of the budget, its commitments and the scope for new developmental spending.
☐ An assessment of staff skills, training and experience to establish the capability of the library service to introduce changes, especially relating to IT.
☐ The motivation of staff and their attitude to new technology is important to the success of any new strategy.

Benefits of carrying out an IT audit

Many library services already have a substantial investment in IT systems. The investment includes not only the hardware and software used in the system but also the staff skills and knowledge acquired through training and experience in using the systems. All of these factors must be taken into account when planning new systems. The larger the legacy of older systems the more difficult it may be to introduce something completely new.

Carrying out an IT audit will produce benefits by:

☐ ensuring effective use of existing systems
☐ maximizing the hardware investment
☐ confirming software compliance
☐ optimizing software licences
☐ providing control of software versions
☐ increasing effectiveness of existing software
☐ protecting assets.

The current position

An audit of existing IT operations can be the starting point for the more detailed consideration of the different parts of an IT strategy. Such an audit is relatively easy to carry out since most of the work involves observation and there should be documents to consult that give a good picture of the current situation. All IT systems currently in use and the information or facilities provided by them should be analysed and the justification for each element outlined. An assessment of their effectiveness will provide a basis for deciding where improvements can be made to benefit the library service. The degree of integration and compatibility will need to be determined. Systems may have been introduced in isolation, often as individual projects at different times when money became available. The development of networking technology has increased the need to bring isolated elements together into an integrated structure.

The resources devoted to current operations, including expenditure on maintenance, replacements and upgrades, consumables, electricity and data links, should be worked out in detail and the relevant budget headings listed. Present and future revenue costs should be evaluated. Any extension of IT facilities will inevitably lead to an increase in revenue expenditure.

The end result should be an outline of the current position, what is required to deal with present shortcomings and the mapping out of a potential improved position for the future.

The IT legacy

In most organizations there will be a history of older IT systems which will influence the service's potential for future change. The question is how far the legacy restrains or discourages further development. Maximum benefit needs to be drawn from past investments, existing strengths need to be properly assessed and weaknesses overcome. An objective overview of the current situation which is agreed by all managers must be obtained so that any limitations that might prevent new systems being introduced can be defined. A consensus must be reached on changes to take place and on objectives that are not achievable with the existing systems.

Existing IT culture

IT systems have often been introduced by experts who may have come to dominate the IT policies of the library service. This may have negative effects upon change. There may be a tendency to force new systems to fit existing data structures. Innovation may be restricted by an inability to use new suppliers if IT is tied into an existing supplier by large investments in the past. IT staff may be too close to the present system to be able to take an objective view of alternatives. They may not want to relearn many basic tasks, which could follow the introduction of a different system. Knowledge is power and technical experts can cloud inconvenient requests with a smoke-screen of unchallengeable details about a system's capabilities.

IT staff are often under-resourced and spend much of their time on routine maintenance with little time to monitor new developments. The converse of this scenario is one in which individual users have been allowed too much control. There may be a proliferation of preferred systems and suppliers, little quality control of data, widely varying skills and experience and the problems of new staff faced with an unfamiliar system which only the original user understood. Much duplication of effort can occur and there may be widely varying rates of development in different parts of the organization which prevents any useful transfer of information. Users themselves may be spending valuable professional time sorting out their own problems because their systems are not centrally supported.

IT policies

Existing policies that apply to IT systems should be examined to see if they are adequate. Increasing the overall IT investment will inevitably mean changing some of these policies as the systems become more complex and more important.

The following policy areas may need to be examined:

☐ existence and enforcement of standards
☐ security, including access to systems and accountability
☐ licensing arrangements for software, CD-ROMs etc.
☐ user support
☐ responsibilities for IT resources
☐ suppliers: service standards, contracts, financial health, discounts, tendering
☐ technology agreements with staff and unions
☐ corporate agreements, corporate standards etc.

Chapter 8 includes more detail on policies to be included in the building blocks of the IT strategy.

IT management

The management of the existing IT investment must also be examined. This will include the current IT staffing structure, including any work undertaken by staff who are not designated as IT workers but whose jobs have become largely devoted to it. An analysis of the work done connected with it will probably reveal that far more time is devoted to it than might be supposed from the organizational chart.

Other questions which might be asked include:

☐ What level in the organizational hierarchy is the current IT staffing?
☐ Is the style of the existing IT staff mainly proactive or reactive?
☐ What are the main demands and priorities on staff?
☐ How well is the IT function integrated into the library service?
☐ How is maintenance managed?
☐ How is the supply of consumables managed?
☐ Are monitoring and diagnostic tasks carried out effectively?
☐ How well are administration tasks dealt with?

The assessment of current practice on these issues is important. Policies for IT and the management of IT are necessary parts of the overall IT strategy. A more detailed discussion of management requirements is undertaken in Chapter 8.

Assessment of human assets

IT skills

An IT audit needs to include an assessment of IT skills within the library service. Some of the questions which need to be answered include:

☐ What are the attitudes of staff to IT?
☐ Are staff skills and expertise utilized effectively?
☐ How widely is knowledge spread in the library service?
☐ Are there pockets of expertise among closed groups?
☐ Are some groups or individuals way ahead of others?
☐ What expertise is there in software and the development of applications?

IT training

The existing training policy should be examined and training facilities assessed. There are a number of questions which need to asked including:

☐ Is IT training generally in-house or external?
☐ What facilities exist for in-house IT training?
☐ Who is responsible for training management?
☐ Who carries out the training?
☐ What areas are covered in existing training?
☐ What areas are neglected?
☐ Which staff are trained and which are not?
☐ How effective is the training?
☐ Is the training budget adequate?
☐ Is training part of the strategic management plan?

Physical assets and liabilities
Assessment of physical constraints

The physical assets of the library service and the suitability for IT must be assessed. The existing physical infrastructure of a library service is one of the limiting factors in the implementation of any IT strategy. Provision may be needed for expenditure on new furniture, altering the layout of buildings or structural work before new IT systems can be effectively introduced. Few buildings were designed with modern IT systems in mind but have to be adapted to them. There may be difficulties in installing IT systems in some buildings because of the construction materials used. Some older buildings may contain asbestos which must not be disturbed. Some libraries are listed buildings and permission may have to be sought for any alterations or additions. The cost of carrying out work on such buildings can be high.

Problems of space and possible shortages in the future must be considered. If the library is or expects to be experiencing a growth in demand for services including space then the physical constraints of existing buildings must be assessed. IT equipment requires a substantial amount of space for its accommodation and for access by users and maintenance staff.

Few library services operate on a single site, far fewer in a single building. The distance between buildings may be many miles. This factor must be taken into account when planning the introduction of IT systems.

Accommodation

In assessing the limitations of the accommodation for IT systems in existing buildings a number of questions need to be considered:

☐ Can the accommodation be adapted for the installation of new equipment, including cabling?
☐ Are there special problems with older buildings, such as a lack of conduits for wiring?
☐ Do modern buildings have problematic concrete floors or partition walls?
☐ Is there sufficient space to house equipment to conform with health and safety requirements?
☐ Will buildings have to be closed while installation work is

taking place?
- [ ] Will existing fittings have to be moved to accommodate the IT equipment?
- [ ] Will the introduction of modern furniture for IT affect the character of an older building?
- [ ] Will extra security precautions be required to protect valuable new equipment?

Geography

The location and distribution of sites in a library service has an important impact upon the IT infrastructure, communications, support and effectiveness. Building a network to link remote and central sites is usually one of the major tasks in implementing an IT strategy. The exact nature of the network will depend upon the distance between sites, the feasibility of using leased lines, the amount of traffic expected on the network from each site and the facilities required at each site. Most solutions are a compromise between the facilities provided and their relative cost.

Each site must be assessed individually with a proper site survey. This may have to be carried out by a specialist or by a team, including an electrician and a network designer. Suppliers of large systems such as library circulation systems will undertake this as part of their contract before installation.

Information and systems modelling

This is less complicated than it sounds. The result of the research into internal systems should be a detailed picture of the present situation, a set of ideas for how information should flow in the library service and how IT systems could fit together to meet the future needs of the service. This can be sketched in outline but research needs to be carried out into possible solutions to the needs of the library service before a final plan is drawn up. This is described in Chapter 6.

The strategy will eventually produce a list of prioritized IT applications which link directly into the library service's main objectives and a portfolio of systems that need to be introduced and developed in the near future. Chapters 7 and 8 describe how this is built up.

References

1   March, James G. quoted by Feldman, S., 'The Online World 1996 Conference', *Information today*, December 1996, 14.
2   Lovecy, Ian, 'From dream to reality: the politics of an IT strategy', *British journal of academic librarianship*, 6 (2), 1991, 85–91.

6 The external context

If it works, it's out of date.

Beer[1]

Objectives
- ☐ **Examine external threats and opportunities**
- ☐ **Assess pressures for change from external bodies**
- ☐ **Examine the state of the art in IT**
- ☐ **Look at practice in other libraries and information services**
- ☐ **Gather information through research, visits and workshops**
- ☐ **Identify the main development aims.**

The Environment
Environmental scanning

Scanning is the process of gathering information from outside the organization which might have an impact upon its short-term or long-term future. Some organizations, especially government agencies, organize this on a formal basis and employ sophisticated techniques to analyse the information. Most organizations leave it to individual managers to keep themselves informed about their own area of responsibility and this can be a hit-and-miss affair.

A new project is more likely to succeed if research has been undertaken beforehand and this requires a more formal and systematic approach. Developing an IT strategy is an important task and the person responsible must be well informed about the state of the art in IT, about developments and projects elsewhere and about the general issues of concern to management that may influence the strategy. Scanning is likely to reveal both threats and opportunities.

Luffman divides environmental scanning into several main components for easier analysis.[2] These are the economic, social, technological and political environments, each of which has particular factors that may influence the organization.

The external environment needs to be examined in detail to assess:

☐ pressures that can result from interactions with other organizations
☐ the current state of the art of IT systems in the marketplace and under development
☐ opportunities for the library service
☐ any future threats or obstacles that may arise from external events and policies.

Many, if not all, of these factors will be beyond the control of the individual organization, although some influence may be exerted upon other organizations if the links are strong enough. In most circumstances the organization can go only with the general flow of events. The task is to acquire a good sense of the direction of these events.

Threats and opportunities

Strengths and weaknesses will have been identified as part of the assessment of the internal operation and management of the library service. There is also the task of listing possible future strategies which can provide a defence against external threats or exploit the potential of any opportunities that might occur.

Some changes may be seen as both possible threats or opportunities, depending upon the outlook of the organization. Education is becoming oriented around a portfolio of student needs rather than being based upon a standard curriculum, delivered in modules via a virtual online system rather than delivered in classrooms according to a timetable. There has been a rapid growth in the numbers of part-time and mature students as the need for continual updating of skills has grown. Courses are already being delivered via the Internet, which has the potential to become a universal educational facility. Universities may see this as both a threat and an opportunity.

Threats

The threat of potential competition from other organizations using IT to move into the same field of provision must be assessed. This is particularly true in the changing world of IT where boundaries between products and services, organizations and delivery systems are being broken down or are becoming blurred. Television, for example, is likely to change from being a purely broadcast service to one in which interactive information retrieval is possible. Information is becoming more of a location-free resource rather than being dependent upon physical stores such as libraries. The Internet has shown the way towards the seamless integration of personal, organizational and external information. External information may be local, regional, national or international and still be accessible in the same way with the same universal interface. This information is being provided by means of a complex network of systems accessible through domestic computers, public kiosks, institutional and commercial facilities. How will the library respond to such threats?

Some threats might be obvious, such as a cut in the budget. Others may be less easy to assess, such as the effect of increased computer usage in the home or in the library on the borrowing of library books.

The threats might also give rise to questions such as:

- What happens if we do not introduce a system everyone else is using?
- Will we fall far behind if we do not follow this new trend in library service?
- Will this new system make some of our functions obsolete?
- Will this new commercial service compete for our users?

Opportunities

There will be opportunities as well as threats which can be identified in the external world. Opportunities may arise from the introduction of new computer techniques, from improved software or communications technology, from alliances with peer organizations for joint developments, from grants and external funding for IT projects.

A recent example of an opportunity has been the eagerness of the EU to fund IT developments in a wide range of organizations in order to push Europe ahead of global competitors in the race for industrial and commercial dominance. A great deal of money has become available for cooperative projects for libraries under the Electronic Libraries Programme and the Fourth Framework Telematics Programme.[3,4]

Research should provide ideas for new applications in the library. Looking for ideas from other libraries in the same field or in different fields can be productive. What should be avoided is the 'me too' approach – introducing new ideas simply because other library services have them. Any ideas should be rigorously assessed for their relevance to the overall aims of the library service. New applications can improve services and also provide useful learning experiences for staff, thus building up the overall knowledge base in the library service and increasing the level of competence in the use of IT systems.

Opportunities which might present themselves should be looked at carefully and subjected to detailed scrutiny. Questions should be asked about their practicality or their viability. Among the questions would be:

☐ Would this help us improve our existing services?
☐ What new services could we develop based upon this new technology?
☐ What benefit would users derive from this development?
☐ Would this make us more efficient?
☐ Would this help reduce costs?
☐ Can we find the necessary resources to participate?

External pressures
External influences

All organizations are dependent upon other organizations for successful operation. There are many potential pressures from cooperation, competition, external policies and legislation, pressure groups and the background of public opinion that will have an influence upon the way a library operates. External influences can be a significant influence on the organization, pressuring it to conform to certain standards or norms in its external dealings. One example for libraries might be the acceptance of MARC standard data from suppliers. Whenever a library decides to go against the norm it inevitably incurs extra costs, its room for manoeuvre becomes restricted and its ability to cooperate with its peers may be reduced by its uniqueness. The pressures may be benign rather than threatening but they must be taken into account.

Among the external pressures which libraries may need to consider are those from:

☐ the parent or funding body
☐ government policies
☐ national bodies
☐ regional groups
☐ professional bodies
☐ information and service suppliers
☐ peer organizations
☐ local bodies
☐ community organizations
☐ businesses
☐ potential sponsors and grant-making bodies
☐ competition, including IT-based systems such as the Internet
☐ trades unions.

The funding body

Libraries usually operate as part of larger organizations such as private companies, local authorities, universities and other academic institutions, government departments and health authorities. Their budgets are usually set by the parent body. These may be subject to the vagaries of funding experienced by the parent body itself or affected by the conflicting demands for resources of its different divisions. In some cases, budgets are dependent upon political decisions and there may be a degree of uncertainty from one year to the next about the exact size of the budget. The tendency in recent years has been for budgets to be tightly controlled. In the public sector regular cuts have been made in revenue budgets as public expenditure generally has been reduced by government spending limits. Libraries usually have only a limited amount of influence in this process.

IT, however, has become a political issue at a national and an international level and this has provided some scope for libraries to exert influence locally. No organization wants to fall behind in the modern world, especially one in which failures and shortcomings are so often highlighted in the media. The formulation of a coherent IT strategy which can be presented and justified to the funding body is likely to be more successful than individual initiatives which, although important, can seem like a never-ending list of unrelated demands.

The policies of the funding body will be equally as important as the budget it provides. There may be policies concerning equal opportunities, customer care, performance indicators, quality services, value for money, the use of IT equipment generally, confidentiality of information, security, relationships with businesses or community organizations, tendering, contracting out, preferred suppliers etc. A good general knowledge of these policies is important if the IT strategy is to reflect the values of the organization.

Government policies

Government policies relating directly to libraries are rare, though other policies can have a significant effect upon the way libraries operate. Recently, there have been a number of reports such as the Public Libraries Review which have had an impact upon the evaluation of IT. Both indicate that IT strategies are necessary.[5] The recent report on the electronic delivery of government services suggested a role for libraries in disseminating information through public kiosks.[6]

Public Lending Right depends upon the collection of statistics of issues of book titles from computerized library systems at selected public libraries. The sample libraries are changed from time to time. Copyright legislation affects all libraries and there are moves towards more rigorous definitions of how copyright will be applied to electronic information made available on CD-ROMs and across networks.

The problem of access to pornographic material on the Internet has raised the possibility of government-imposed censorship. This may not be possible on an international level and there may be moves towards making individual library services liable for policing their own users.

National bodies

There are many bodies operating at a national level that may have an influence on the policies of libraries. There are several local government organizations that lobby government on behalf of their members. The Association of Metropolitan Authorities (AMA) has frequently commented upon public library services and has backed calls for public libraries to be linked to the information superhighway. A number of educational bodies represent the interests of universities and colleges. One of the most significant reports for university libraries issued recently was the Follett Report which made recommendations for major changes in IT provision in universities.[7]

Regional groups

Regional groups of one sort or another are becoming more common, particularly in relation to applications for funding from Europe or from the government for regional economic development projects. Such groupings might provide an opportunity to become involved in a larger project which would not otherwise be feasible. There may be pressure to participate by the alternative threat of being excluded from a new development. Political considerations as well as practical ones usually have to be taken into account in joint projects. In north west England, for example, the North West Inter-Regional Information Society Initiative (NWIRISI) has been active in developing plans for funding IT projects in partnership with similar regions in other European countries as part of a general EU scheme. Libraries have been invited to become involved in some of the projects.

Professional bodies

The Library Association is increasingly taking upon itself the role of negotiator on behalf of libraries. For example, it put forward a bid for Millennium funding to connect public libraries to the information superhighway. In doing so, it requested the support of library authorities, effectively committing them to the proposal before any of them had seen the details. Although the bid was turned down, public libraries may find themselves under pressure to accept an alternative system that might not have been their own choice. Even those which do not sign up to a proposal may find that eventually they have to adopt whatever system is accepted by the majority.

Information and service suppliers

Publishers are producing more and more electronic products as alternatives to printed materials. In some specialist areas such as business information there is a steady migration away from print and microfiche products, which are relatively expensive to produce, towards CD-ROM and the Internet. Some directories and company financial database products that were formerly available in print are now exclusively electronic. Publishers are obviously eager to move towards electronic provision as a means of cutting their production costs. Users are thus pressured into adopting the systems needed to access this specialized information or to cease providing it.

Electronic products offer many advantages over printed materials and this in itself is often reason enough to consider an electronic version of an important reference work. There may be opportunities for enhancing services, for providing better security and for providing wider access through CD-ROM networking.

Library suppliers who provide an intermediary service between libraries and publishers have also adopted IT systems for stock control. Libraries that buy in bulk from particular suppliers can also obtain bibliographic records for the items they purchase and thus save themselves effort in cataloguing. Suppliers will generally want to provide such data in standard formats and library systems must be capable of accepting this data if they are to take advantage of the time savings.

Peer organizations

The assessment of a library's position in the external environment is an important part of the scanning process. A library must identify its position in relation to similar libraries in its own field, comparing progress with its peers. Much of the impetus for change comes from monitoring the progress of similar organizations and the innovations they produce. It is usually quite easy to determine where one's own library service fits in the league table of similar bodies according to its services, its achievements, its performance and its reputation. Utilizing the tried and tested ideas of others is a safe way of improving services.

Local bodies

There are many local bodies which interact for mutual benefit. Local authorities, chambers of commerce, Training and Enterprise Councils (TECs), educational establishments, health authorities and others may develop formal or informal links to cooperate on joint projects. More and more of these are related to IT. Cable companies in the larger metropolitan areas have formed a number of consortia with local bodies to develop innovative content and interactive services to exploit the potential of optical fibre networks. Even if the library service is not directly involved, the plans of these bodies need to be monitored for possible threats or opportunities. There is a danger that local information may be duplicated or that competing services may be introduced when cooperation between the bodies could prevent this.

Community organizations

A number of community electronic networking projects now exist. These are generally partnerships between voluntary organizations, local authorities, academic institutions, businesses and libraries in local areas. The development of partnerships with local community information providers to develop projects that improve access to electronic information at a local level should be considered as part of the IT strategy. Such projects can help to bring a library service into closer contact with the community as well as forging useful links with community organizations which can be developed further in the future.

Businesses

Private companies indirectly exert the greatest pressure of all as far as IT is concerned. This is because they are such heavy investors in new systems which might give them a competitive advantage that they are the main driving force for change in the marketplace. Libraries exert little influence upon what has become a global market for IT products and services and can only follow the trends as best as they can. Many articles in computing journals contain case studies of the use of IT by leading companies that are useful guides to what is possible.

Partnerships with local companies may also be possible. IT companies may be willing to take part in projects that enable them to demonstrate new products. Various telematics initiatives by the EU have provided scope for such partnerships. In the USA companies such as Microsoft have become involved in large-scale projects with libraries and educational institutions to test services based upon their software and hardware products.

Potential sponsors and grant-making bodies

Some local and national companies may be prepared to sponsor IT projects as a way of associating themselves with worthwhile public projects. BT has specific community programmes, Nynex has been involved with several local projects in its franchise region in north west England to develop the interactive use of cable. A search for possible local sponsors may be worth considering for some IT projects as part of the IT strategy.

Similarly, a search for possible grant aid should be undertaken for some projects. Some larger organizations have units that coordinate this type of activity and libraries should take advantage of their facilities. Grants for IT projects have many restrictions and conditions attached to them but more and more are becoming available. The EU has provided many millions of ECUs for IT projects in libraries in the last few years. The British Library has also provided research money for innovative projects. Although lottery money does not yet seem to be available for IT projects in libraries the situation may change in the future if there is enough political pressure to vary the rules.

Competition

Libraries face many potential competitors in the evolving information society. Commercial companies who see potential profits in electronic information provision are experimenting with new services. Internet providers and services such as Compuserve and America Online have already shown the potential for generating large cash flows from electronic information. Telecommunications and cable companies are setting up pilot projects to provide access to information and other services through public kiosks and interactive television channels. Cybercafes and other outlets have introduced an element of direct competition for Internet access. Libraries will want to assess such services to see whether they can provide access to them for their users and whether they can participate in the services themselves, perhaps as information providers.

As well as competition for service provision, libraries face the prospect of their traditional materials base being undermined by electronic publishing on the Internet. Many journals are becoming available in both print and electronic forms, some are available only electronically, others are finding print to be an increasingly expensive option. Conventional printed materials are becoming more and more expensive to purchase whilst book funds are generally decreasing. Libraries are thus faced with a gradual erosion of their physical assets and will increasingly find themselves competing for users who can access electronic information from a variety of outlets.

Trades unions

Although much reduced in influence nationally, trades unions do have a role in protecting the interests of their members at a local level. New technology agreements operate in many organizations such as local authorities and academic institutions. Where IT is likely to lead to reductions in staffing, changes to structures, the creation of new posts and the need for new skills, then trades unions may need to be consulted or informed. Agreements may be needed to ensure a smooth introduction of new systems.

State of the art
Aims

In considering the impact of the external environment on the library service there are a number of distinct aims. One of the main tasks is to assess the current state of the art in IT. The assessment will aim to:

☐ list IT products and systems that offer an advantage and fit in with long-term strategy
☐ identify products that will improve efficiency
☐ identify systems that will improve services

☐ identify best practice for IT applications internally
☐ get a feel for the best products and suppliers
☐ develop an overview of the wide range of IT systems available.

This must also involve a degree of prediction because the implementation of the strategy may come several months, possibly as long as one or two years, after the strategy has been produced depending upon the finance available, although the intention should be to implement as soon as possible. IT systems are changing and developing so rapidly that products rarely stay on the market for more than a year before they are superseded by something more powerful and advanced. The aim should be to try to install IT systems which are up to date at the time of implementation rather than those which were current at the time of investigation. Options will need to be kept open to some extent to allow for any delay in implementation.

Another aim is to develop an understanding of how other organizations have made use of IT to improve their performance and how they have coped with the problems of adapting to new systems. Accompanying any introduction of a new IT system will have been changes in the roles and attitudes of staff in the organization. There are few instances of IT being introduced without an effect upon existing organizational structures and relationships. These effects must be understood and provision made for them as part of the implementation plan.

The process of scanning the environment does not take place in isolation but should be going on in the background while other parts of the IT strategy are being formulated. There may already be well-informed individuals in the library service who can be called upon to make recommendations and offer guidance on the latest systems or techniques.

The IT marketplace

There is a plethora of IT systems in the marketplace and the range is constantly and rapidly growing. Some systems will be more suitable than others for a particular library service. In order to keep up with the constant changes taking place, some kind of current awareness programme is required. Whether this is formally organized or informal, the first aim should be to gain a broad overview of what exists in the marketplace. The next stage is to concentrate the search for applications that would have real benefit for the library service. The systems and products available should be evaluated against the library service's real needs. The process is thus one of filtering out applications which it is realistic to introduce from the mass of those which may seem exciting and even futuristic but which may have only a slight chance of succeeding.

The main problem in introducing a new system is almost certainly the reaction of staff to the new technology. What might look attractive and straightforward in the pages of a computer magazine may involve a complete change of culture in an organization. Technology imposes its own rules on the way people work and demands that the rules be followed stringently if the benefits are to be fully realized. Trying to introduce too many changes at once, which would involve a mass of learning curves, would only lead to confusion and disillusionment. Any changes should be gradual and follow a logical plan of implementation, allowing enough time for proper assimilation.

Current practice in other libraries

Detailed scanning, for example on the Internet, of projects under way in libraries shows a very diverse range of activities. Even where one particular activity can be isolated there are different methods being used by libraries in different countries. Despite this proliferation there are many common threads and libraries often reach a consensus about the best approach. One example of this is the production of Web pages by libraries. Many libraries are installing their own Web servers and have developed rules for different aspects of the process. There are Internet pages which list policies devised by US public libraries for allowing library users to access the Internet from public terminals. These could serve with a minimum adaptation as convenient guides for libraries in other countries.

Products and systems being introduced by libraries at the moment which may need to be considered include:

□ computer-assisted or open learning
□ interactive multimedia
□ remote access by users
□ NCs or network computers
□ smart cards

☐ expanded Internet services
☐ electronic publishing and document delivery
☐ Electronic Data Interchange (EDI)
☐ Broadband communications such as the Integrated Services Digital Network (ISDN) and Asynchronous Transfer Mode (ATM)
☐ video, including video-conferencing
☐ voice-mail and voice input.

A more detailed list of essential elements for library systems will be given in Chapter 7.

Policies and management practices

Of equal importance to the hardware and software, systems and networks other libraries have installed is an examination of the policies regarding IT and how IT is managed, often overlooked in the heady excitement of assessing the physical elements of an IT infrastructure. In many organizations these intangible elements may not be documented and details may thus be difficult to obtain. Articles in professional journals may provide some descriptions, with case studies providing the most useful insights.

More detail about these elements are provided in Chapter 8.

Methodology
Research

There are many avenues of research to be explored and the work is best carried out by being divided up among a number of team members. The work will involve literature searches for information on specific topics plus a great deal of browsing in current literature including professional journals, trade magazines and the IT press generally. There are many magazines devoted to both business and consumer use of computers, most reiterating the same messages and covering the same products. These magazines are useful for informative articles about new technologies, for comparative testing of similar products, for coverage of new, often obscure developments, and for the advertising copy which gives a good indication of who the leading suppliers are. Magazines and advertisers, however, are in the business of selling products and the hype given to much new software and hardware must not be taken too seriously. Some publications attempt to provide objective assessments of new products and give detailed accounts of tests or opinions of users, in the style of the Consumer Association's *Which?* magazine. *What to buy for business*, for example, recently published a critical survey of portable computers.[8] Reports of tests can be informative but should not be taken at face value. The next stage on from identifying potential products should be to try them out.

Internet sources

The Internet is one of the most important sources of information on developments in IT in library services and computer developments generally. The World Wide Web has become the most extensive source of information on products, suppliers, techniques, new research and funding opportunities. Software in particular is heavily promoted with demonstrations and free versions available for downloading. Most computer companies have Web pages with information about their products. Search engines such as Alta Vista or Yahoo can be used to identify pages quickly on particular subjects such as video conferencing or network computers.

Information on specific themes may be obtained by monitoring newsgroups and bulletin boards, although this can be a slow and frustrating experience unless the right sources are accessed. Even then, much of the information may be random and trivial in content.

Of more interest are listservers, which send messages such as newsletters via e-mail to personal mailboxes but can have the same discussion facilities as newsgroups. Messages are posted by individuals to a central server, which then posts them on to all other subscribers' e-mail addresses. As well as providing information for current awareness purposes listservers can point to useful contacts from whom further information and expert advice may be sought. A number of listservers for librarians exist such as lis-pub-libs for public libraries, lis-elib for the electronic libraries programme, both of which are available in the UK on the Mailbase system.[9] There are many US listservers such as web4lib, which covers Internet issues in libraries. The Web server Library-Oriented Lists and Electronic Serials provides a long list of possibilities.[10]

Professional contacts

Contacts with other people working on IT in libraries and other organizations are essential. A great deal of useful advice can be obtained from people who have already had experience in implementing systems and know about the pitfalls and problems involved. No amount of reading and talking to suppliers can match the real-life experiences of those who have struggled with the introduction of new systems. There are many established user groups for leading suppliers' systems and products which may be able to give advice and warn of potential pitfalls.

Visits

Site visits to library services which have already implemented systems where they can be seen in operation and where people can be questioned about their experiences can be useful. Suppliers may arrange visits to sites where their latest systems have been successfully installed. Visits to suppliers' premises can be useful also but often provide a one-sided view of the products, which are presented in the most favourable circumstances. The visits can serve to give an overall impression of the professionalism and the competence of the supplier by looking at the way things are organized and how questions are dealt with. The degree of openness and the willingness to deal with any difficult and searching questions will give an idea of the sincerity of the supplier. Demonstrations may be useful to obtain an idea of the capabilities of a system but those that involve test databases give only a partial impression. True speed and performance should be assessed only by trying out a real working system already installed in a similar organization.

Visits to exhibitions can provide some background knowledge and occasionally new ideas. The demonstrations, though, are often well prepared and presented to a standard formula, often by trained presenters rather than experts in the systems themselves. Some exhibitions are so popular and crowded that it is impossible to see more than a few products in any detail. Preplanning is essential if the visit is to be productive. Exhibitions might be seen as an interim stage between reading about a product and testing it out on a live system. Unfortunately, exhibitions may not to be held at times convenient for the planning timetable of an IT strategy and cannot be relied upon as the main source of information.

Workshops and brainstorming

Using the expertise and knowledge that exists within the organization is an obvious route to obtain ideas. Libraries may be large enough in themselves to call upon considerable in-house knowledge or skills in IT. If not, it may be possible to utilize skills within the wider organization. This process may be combined to some extent with assessing the needs of staff and users within the library service for IT. Workshops may be arranged to generate ideas for the introduction of new systems and facilities. Suggestions can be followed up with further research. Brainstorming sessions may be useful in stimulating a flow of ideas and focusing on the main priorities for development and improvement. There may be a need for a series of workshops to obtain a wide cross-section of views and ideas from managers and operational staff.

Identifying the main development aims
Key issues

The work done in acquiring an overview of the library service and its needs, the external environment and the opportunities available should lead into the identification of key issues for the development of the library service. Different libraries will give emphasis to different developments. There will, however, be some common issues for all libraries, the most important of which is interconnection of networks. Libraries and information services cannot operate in isolation and their ability to network together will become more crucial in the future. Networking will be the number one key issue for most libraries. There will be others.

Defining the options

Having identified the key issues, the next task is to define the options for development. There may be more than one way of achieving an objective. The provision of Internet access, for example, might be achieved through a number of standalone computers with minimal security. It might be provided through ISDN connections to a limited number of users on a local area network (LAN) or it might be provided across a large network via a dedicated line with firewalls to protect the network. The different options need to be considered and possibly costed for optimum value for money. Chapter 7 describes the different physical elements that need to be considered as part of the strategy process.

References

1 Beer, Stafford, *Brain of the firm*, 2nd edn, London, Wiley, 1981.
2 Luffman, G. and others, *Strategic management an analytical approach*, Oxford, Blackwell, 1996, 35–41.
3 *Electronic Libraries Programme.* **http://www.dlib.org/dlib/december95/briefings/12uk.html**
4 DG XIII, *Fourth framework programme, call for proposals: libraries*, Brussels, European Commission, 1993.
5 Department of National Heritage, *Reading the future, a review of public libraries in England*, March 1997.
6 Chancellor of the Duchy of Lancaster, *Government.direct, a prospectus for the electronic delivery of government services*, Cm 3438, London, HMSO, November 1996.
7 Higher Education funding Council for England, *Joint Funding Council's Libraries Funding Review Group: report*, HEFCE, Bristol, 1993. **http://ukoln.bath.ac.uk/follett/follett_report.html**
8 'Up, up and away – portable computer article', *What to buy for business*, March 1997, 6–49.
9 *Mailbase.* **http://mailbase.ac.uk/**
10 *Library-oriented lists and electronic serials.* **http://info.lib.uh.edu/liblists/home.htm**

7 Elements of the strategy – physical infrastructure

No manager ever got fired for buying IBM.

IBM advertising slogan

Objectives

- Assess the need for networks, hardware, software
- Look at the potential of different media and online facilities
- Examine broadband services
- Examine the library's role as an electronic information provider
- Produce an infrastructure plan for the library service.

The physical infrastructure
Building blocks

The physical components of IT can be regarded as building blocks for the construction of a customized infrastructure for the library service. Every service will have different needs and different ideas about how to build such an infrastructure. This chapter gives an outline of the main physical components in an IT strategy. It does not intend to provide a comprehensive guide to building a network and does not detail all the network topologies, devices, protocols, and standards that need to be considered. There are many books and articles on networks which may be consulted for further details.

Expertise

The production of a detailed plan for an IT infrastructure is a specialized task which may require assistance from external consultants. Networks in particular can be complex to plan and build. Library systems suppliers will design networks as part of their system implementation plans. Technical help may be available from corporate computer units. What is needed for the task is a high degree of technical knowledge and confidence that the design will work in practice.

Networks
Backbones

Electronic networks are vitally important and in the near future they will form the backbone of information provision in most organizations. They will provide vital links between organizations and the economies of nations will depend on them in the forthcoming information society. Without them, most organizations will be unable to function effectively in the modern world. The library service's network, if there is one, should be assessed for its suitability for future development. The network must be flexible enough to provide a wide and increasing range of services for users and staff. If no network exists it is likely that the installation of one that will serve the library service for the next five to ten years will prove the single most important element of the IT strategy. Networks must be capable of coping with heavier and heavier loads of information traffic, especially from the use of multimedia. The bandwidth of the different elements of the network must be sufficiently broad to allow access by many simultaneous users without an unacceptable decrease in response times.

The backbone cable specified for modern organizations is optical fibre with a bandwidth of 100 Mb/s. From this backbone individual rooms and devices may be connected by Ethernet cable running at 10 Mb/s. In the future this latter is unlikely to be adequate for multimedia applications such as video conferencing, and recabling may be needed with 100 Mb/s Ethernet. This escalation in bandwidth demand should be taken into account when new systems are being installed. Some libraries are already beginning to install network cable with the greater capacity. The recently opened Learning Resources Centre at South Bank University has done this and also has links to a local cable company.[1] Any work done in cabling should ensure that future recabling can be carried out using existing conduits and cableways to minimize costs.

Local area networks

The simplest network may be a local area network, which connects a number of PCs in a room or in one building. Once a LAN has been established, many facilities can be added to it for the benefit of all users. These range from shared devices such as fax machines, modems and printers to servers for documents, images and software.

In a library this may provide LAN users with access to basic elements such as:

☐ the library's catalogue database
☐ CD-ROM servers for bibliographic and other information
☐ gateways to access online hosts, book suppliers, the Internet etc.
☐ in-house databases such as an internal telephone directory or periodicals holdings
☐ the interlending system
☐ shared colour printing facilities.

Some libraries may also have further facilities such as:

☐ internal and external e-mail
☐ an Intranet
☐ fax on the network
☐ management information
☐ document servers
☐ bulletin boards or discussion groups
☐ image banks
☐ video conferencing.

The LAN is essentially a cable that links all the devices together and allows them to communicate with central servers and with each other. The length of the cable is limited and may require extra equipment to boost signals if the length is exceeded. Many buildings need complicated plans to route cable through and around obstacles in the most efficient way. Special equipment such as bridges, routers and splitters may be needed to overcome technical problems. The work involved in designing a network requires expertise and should not be undertaken by an amateur. A comprehensive site survey will be needed to assess the physical work for cabling and electricity supplies as well as designing the cable route. Accurate diagrams of the resulting network and the devices attached to it are essential for efficient management and maintenance.

Interconnections

In large organizations there may be several independent LANs operating in different buildings or in different divisions. These may be interconnected to form a larger network. Access by other parts of the organization, outside organizations and individuals to the library's network, if any, should be assessed.

In Manchester, for example, the City Council Leader's office has been provided with access to the Central Library LAN, for accessing information such as national newspapers on CD-ROM. This has been achieved by utilizing an existing optical fibre connection between the library LAN and the Council's corporate network. The link to the corporate network enables the library to access corporate databases such as the Human Resources database and the Financial Management system. It will also allow the library to provide further information services to officers and members of the City Council in the future. Terminals on the library LAN with the appropriate browser software and permission can now also access the Council's Intranet server, which has an A–Z of Council services, a searchable directory of Council staff and a growing range of internal Council information.

This convenient connection is possible because of the close proximity of the town hall to the central library. For more remote connections cable would be expensive to install and different solutions would be needed. Existing data lines would need to be rented from the main telecommunications providers.

Wide area networks

Many library services have such data lines connected as wide area networks (WANs), allowing remote branches to link to a central system for issuing and discharging lending items. The links can be used for accessing other services too. Some county councils have extensive communications networks which provide council-wide facilities over a large geographical area. These services are currently limited in some rural areas by the infrastructure provided by the established telecommunication and cable companies. The larger urban areas have been comprehensively cabled and libraries there should be able to take advantage of the extended facilities offered by wide-band cable in the near future. In other areas facilities will take longer to establish and services such as ISDN and kilostream may be the only alternatives. These may be adequate for most data traffic now but are unlikely to be able to cope with multimedia traffic in the future. Older X25 connections are generally too slow with a narrow bandwidth inadequate for the transfer of higher volumes of data needed for effective information query and retrieval. In Manchester, all district libraries are now connected to the central library LAN by kilostream lines with ISDN backup and have online public access catalogue (OPAC) terminals for searching the centrally located catalogue and CD-ROMs. The distinction between WANs and LANs is gradually disappearing as network speeds increase.

The strategy will involve investigating the most cost-effective way to develop the communications structure, taking account of the need for access to expanding corporate and departmental systems and external information sources. Factors such as the availability of lines, speed and bandwidth, costs, reliability and security need to be assessed. The higher the bandwidth the higher the cost, although costs are decreasing over time.

The aim should be to provide access wherever possible to the full range of information sources available, preferably from multifunctional terminals and to ensure that there is in remote sites the same quality of access to information as in a central HQ. Access should be extended eventually to external users, e.g. council members and officers from different departments in a local authority, researchers in an academic institution, suppliers, teleworkers, cooperative partners, project teams, external organizations and individuals.

Further improvement of the library's computer network to provide access for users to more facilities is likely to be one of the main areas for IT development.

External access

Providing access to the library network to external users to improve their access to information and to enable them to carry out research more effectively and more conveniently from their own terminals may be another priority. This facility is steadily being extended in Manchester, where links from the library LAN to satellite libraries operated by the library service on behalf of town hall departments such as city solicitors have been provided. Few library services have yet provided remote access for their staff for teleworking but this could become more common in the future.

Hardware
Platforms

Hardware is often described in terms of platforms upon which an IT infrastructure is built. This may be divided into mainframes, UNIX-based open systems, proprietary systems and desktop machines. Whatever hardware is in use it must be checked for Year 2000 compliancy and replaced if it is not.

Mainframes

These are still in use by many organizations including universities, local authorities and large commercial companies. Some have large databases which are difficult to transfer on to other platforms. The problems of accessing so-called legacy data effectively is gradually being overcome by a new generation of intermediary software which can provide a Web-based searching interface to cover up the old, unfriendly proprietary system. Although much reduced in price and size, modern mainframes still serve well for reliability, robustness and proven performance. They can handle large amounts of data quickly and are at the heart of many operational systems that handle large volumes of transactions, especially online systems. Most libraries, however, have migrated from corporate mainframes to their own in-house systems for transaction-intensive online operations such as issuing and discharging library materials.

Proprietary systems

In-house systems may be proprietary systems, especially older systems. Library suppliers originally developed their own systems as turnkey systems with no intention of running anything else on the computers used. There was no need to provide open systems facilities. Some libraries will have such legacy systems for the foreseeable future. These systems often require special environmental conditions to operate effectively and so are usually housed in purpose-built rooms with air and temperature controls. The inflexibility of such systems and the high maintenance costs act as a disincentive for further investment. A strategy plan should include a programme for phasing out such systems.

UNIX-based open systems

Modern library systems are generally UNIX-based, although there are several different types of UNIX. These systems allow a degree of interoperability and the portability of applications and data from one to another. A UNIX machine can run several applications side by side with the main library catalogue database. These systems offer good price/performance comparisons with mainframes. They are easily networked and can utilize common user interfaces such as Windows for ease of use. Most modern library systems are based on this platform.

Network servers

These are midway between the larger UNIX machines and desktops but are becoming more and more powerful and capable of handling online demands from many users. Many are being employed as Web servers on the Internet or on Intranets and their capabilities are developing rapidly in this fast growing environment. Their small size and ease of use are making them likely candidates for the next generation of library system machines. Operating systems such as Windows NT are becoming so powerful, flexible and easy to use that they may replace UNIX in the future. The power of network servers and their ability to serve dozens of simultaneous users makes it possible for resources to be concentrated centrally and called up when needed rather than every terminal needing much expensive software. They also permit the efficient sharing of large amounts of information which are better maintained in centralized and standardized storage.

Desktop machines

It is possible to run an office or a complete library service on a PC or a Mac. Many small businesses have been established on the back of a single desktop computer. Libraries in industrial units and colleges have often automated with one microcomputer. Software is available for circulation control and the development of a catalogue on a PC. Library system suppliers now often offer scaled-down versions of their main systems, especially for smaller libraries with networked terminals served by a more powerful PC acting as a file server. The desktop PC running Windows-based software has become the standard interface for many organizations. Most new software is Windows-based and it is unlikely that this type of interface will change significantly in the near future. Desktop machines can work as standalones with their own software, storage and printing facilities. They can also connect into a LAN with the addition of extra software and network cards. With a modem they can link into external services such as fax, e-mail and the Internet. The desktop PC has become a *de facto* standard to which manufacturers and suppliers must conform if they wish to reach a wide market for their products.

Standalone PCs will often have been purchased for specific tasks. The range of standalone PCs and other equipment in locations throughout the library service needs to be audited. Managers may have been provided with desktop computers with both network access and standalone features.

The following applications are available in many libraries on standalone PCs:

□ office applications
□ DTP and reprographics applications
□ communications facilities
□ online information services including the Internet
□ small in-house databases
□ public access computers
□ open learning
□ multimedia CD-ROMs.

With multifunctional terminals networked together there should be less need to have standalone PCs. The future networking of multimedia systems will become a requirement for most library services as multimedia enriched materials become more widespread. The library strategy will need to pay particular attention to the way in which terminals are to be used. Terminals should be multifunctional but in practice they may become dedicated to particular tasks according to the habits of users.

Peripherals

There are many different input and output devices that can be attached to computers or networks. The most obvious output devices are printers. Shared printing facilities on a network provide savings in capital costs and maintenance. A variety of different types of printer can be made accessible when needed for different tasks such as colour printing, high-quality laser copy for graphics and lower definition text copy. It is difficult to predict in advance where printers should be sited for maximum efficiency and convenience. In practice, the patterns of demand at different service points in libraries will need to be taken into account. Security and confidentiality may be important considerations.

Output devices such as plotters and large-format printers for specialized applications may be needed.

Modems used for connections to remote services such as the Internet may be attached to standalone machines or placed on networks to be called up when needed. The trend is for faster and faster connections to be made and the standard modem speed is continually rising. Slower modems, although much cheaper to purchase, will soon prove expensive to run with information retrieval taking several times longer and telephone bills correspondingly higher. On networks modems are gradually being replaced with ISDN routers or direct Internet connections through Web servers. The type of device used will depend on the number of likely simultaneous users, the amount of data traffic and the total number of connections made each day.

Light pens for reading bar-codes in library books are obvious input devices. Problems can arise with the quality of bar-codes and practical tests are vital to make sure that they will fulfil their requirements in day-to-day operation.

Scanners are popular devices used mainly for capturing digital images for incorporation into multimedia applications, desktop publishing or Web pages. Some have optical character recognition (OCR) software for incorporating scanned text into word-processing. Colour, black and white, high and low definition scanning may be needed for different applications. Although scanners may not be expensive they do require expertise to obtain the best results and this represents another learning curve. Devices of this sort are likely to be required only occasionally and may be better provided in a central facility where trained staff can operate them or provide advice on their use.

Software
Types of software

The traditional distinction between operating software, which makes a computer and its attached devices work, and applications software, which provides users with desktop programs, is becoming blurred. Operating software is becoming easier to use with more user-friendly interfaces. Installation from CD-ROMs has become straightforward. Network software includes both operating and applications features. Graphical User Interface (GUI) programs such as Windows are bundles of programs designed to work together and make the operating system easy to use. Internet browser and server software has added another dimension with the concept of hyperlinking documents. The general trend is towards integrating many separate functions in one large suite. Operating software, network software and applications software are converging in many ways as software producers seek to extend their territories. Whilst this provides more functionality for the user, there is also the problem of dealing with larger upgrades and a bigger learning curve.

Choosing new software is particularly difficult. Not only is the choice increasing but changes to established software take place almost monthly with new, often unfinished upgrades being posted on the Internet for downloading. Many software companies offer free versions in a bid to break into the market. A guarantee should be obtained that any new software purchased is Year 2000 compliant.

The increasing size of software suites is making standard floppy disks almost redundant as the preferred method of delivery. CD-ROM is increasingly used for the distribution of large programs and the manuals that accompany them. This means that a CD-ROM drive is needed for loading software on to a desktop or a network server. In the near future the Internet may become the preferred means of purchasing and obtaining software and provision should be made for this form of delivery for standard software. The abundance of shareware on the Internet means that users are almost certain to demand the facility to download software. A fast Internet connection to a network is the most cost-effective option. The network copy can then be distributed more quickly and cheaply from a network server.

Keeping track of all the software in an organization can be a nightmare. If users are permitted to download software at will from the Internet then control is virtually impossible. Some auditing is required to ensure that licensing conditions are being followed. Internal policies may be needed to control pirate copying and the potential spread of viruses. Stringent controls will be needed where members of the public or outside users are allowed to access software on the library network.

Operating system software

Operating system software ranges from the familiar MS DOS for desktop machines to various proprietary versions of UNIX for LANs. Network software such as Novell Netware has recently been challenged by Windows NT, which is becoming increasingly popular for networks and Intranet use. The rapid changes taking place in network software, the gradual integration of netware with Intranetware and the increasing number of functions being added to what was once very basic software has made the choice more difficult. Industry commentators are unsure whether UNIX, Windows NT or some other software will become the future preference. An early decision may need to be taken on one of the main packages. To some extent the choice may be dictated by the applications on the network. If Windows 95 is standard and Microsoft applications are used extensively then Windows NT may be a logical choice. UNIX will almost certainly need specially trained staff to operate and maintain it.

Applications software

Most applications are usually commercial off-the-shelf packages. The range of applications is enormous and for each application there are likely to be several different producers with similar products with variants for different operating systems. There is some advantage in restricting the range of applications software in an organization in order to be able to provide effective support. This is easier on a network where the software can be distributed from a central point. Many organizations will find that there are many variant editions or versions in use of even the most common software applications such as word-processing. Incompatibility will limit the productivity gains from using such applications. The IT strategy must attempt to create order in the software free-for-all by establishing some control over software applications to ensure that the library service benefits fully from their use.

Basic so-called office software is becoming more complex and sophisticated. Most office work is based upon the use of information that is created and handled in many ways. More and more functions that were once carried out as separate processes or were done on separate pieces of equipment are being transferred on to the desktop computer. For example, fax and telephone-answering software is often provided free with modems. Integrated suites are available with several components that are designed to work together to aid productivity. Networks have provided the opportunity for better communication and sharing of files by groups of workers. The Internet has stimulated the growth of hypertext documents and publishing packages.

Users are likely to demand a wide range of applications software including:

- □ communications: e-mail, fax, voice mail, video conferencing
- □ text processing: word-processing, DTP, Web page and HTML software
- □ number processing: spreadsheets, statistical analysis
- □ information processing and retrieval: databases, Internet and Intranet browsers, CD-ROMs
- □ group working: project planning, groupware
- □ multimedia: graphics, sounds, digital images, video manipulation.

The IT strategy should aim to make the most of the productivity benefits that can be obtained from the effective use of applications software. There may be a need to impose restrictions on the brands and versions of software used to ensure that this happens. In choosing software, training, software support, upgrading policies, licensing agreements and other issues must be taken into account.

Library circulation control systems
Integrated systems

Most library systems suppliers produce integrated issue, discharge, cataloguing and acquisitions systems. Although most libraries now have computerized systems, many are several years old and will eventually have to be replaced. Upgrading a system is becoming less easy because the technology is changing so quickly that modern systems will not run on older equipment. The difficulty of obtaining spare parts and retaining staff who can manage older systems which are effectively obsolete means that replacement will become inevitable. Any substantial new capital investment in a public sector organization is likely to require a tendering procedure under EU law. Replacement may thus mean the migration from one system supplier to another. Any major change needs to be carefully planned well in advance and should form part of any strategy.

OPACs

OPAC terminals are increasingly regarded as essential elements in any library service, providing users with access to the main catalogue to search for, reserve and renew books on loan. Most OPACs are microcomputer-based and are increasingly sophisticated, often providing access to other facilities on the library's network besides the basic library catalogue. The aim should be to provide OPACs at all service points and at other convenient locations outside the library service. The trend towards multifunctional terminals will continue in the future with more intelligent interfaces using hypertext software similar to Web browsers being used as standard to provide access to both internal and external information services.

Although many libraries have undertaken some degree of computerization of their issuing systems and have created online lending catalogues, this process has not yet been exhausted. There are a number of developments which can be undertaken to extend and improve upon basic facilities to provide a better service to library users. Some libraries are experimenting with new features, especially Internet access. Most academic library OPACs are now available on the Internet and further improvements are being tested. COPAC, for example, aims to provide unified access to the online catalogues of many of the largest university research libraries in the UK and Ireland.[2] There is obvious scope for other strategic alliances between libraries.

Self-issuing and return

The introduction of self-issuing terminals at heavily used issuing points to provide a faster service for users is one possibility for improving services. Some libraries have already begun to experiment with this. A recent paper by Stafford describes the results of the introduction of this facility in a university library.[3] This facility should be considered for inclusion in the IT strategy for every large busy library service.

Retrospective conversion

The retrospective conversion of library catalogues, especially where this gives access to unique collections, is essential if the full benefits of information technology are to be realized. Many local collections would be exploited nationally and internationally if they were made more accessible. There are obvious cost implications in doing this and the strategy should take this into account. Plans may be needed for several years into the future. External funding may be the only option if the work is to be undertaken. The possibility of obtaining grants and subsidies may need to be investigated as part of the longer term strategy.

Media
CD-ROMs

Providing a range of CD-ROMs on the library network to meet the demands of users for fast retrieval of newspaper and periodical articles, access to directories and other works of reference is becoming a standard service in many libraries. In Manchester Public Libraries 64 CD-ROM drives provide access to a wide range of general interest and specialized titles across the library network. Although CD-ROMs may be only an interim technology, eventually to be superseded, they have a number of advantages over printed publications:

☐ they can be stored centrally for easier maintenance and security
☐ they offer fast retrieval and flexible searching
☐ they provide large savings on space
☐ convenient printouts can be obtained or data downloaded for personal use
☐ they can be accessed remotely from many different sites.

The use of CD-ROMs either on desktop machines or on networks must be considered as one of the necessary building blocks of an IT infrastructure.

Multimedia

There is scope in most library services for the development of multimedia systems, initially standalone but eventually networked, to take advantage of the educational, entertainment, cultural and information facilities of multimedia.

The provision of a range of multimedia computers for users in libraries must be considered. Facilities for children to use multimedia CD-ROMs have been introduced at a number of sites in Manchester Public Libraries. The provision of multimedia CD-ROMs for loan to users will become more important as more titles are published and the number of home multimedia machines increases. In Manchester this service now operates from the central library and two of the larger district libraries.

Online information access

Internet

Demand for access to external sources of information is likely to grow as library budgets diminish and printed materials become too expensive to acquire. Online electronic information sources are increasing in number and becoming more interactive. The most obvious example of this is the Internet. At present a crude mixture of services, the Internet is a pointer to much more sophisticated services which will become available in the near future.

The provision of access for library users to external electronic information systems such as the Internet should be provided either free or for a reasonable cost. Although some users may have access at home many will not and will require access from a library. Web servers that can provide Internet access across the entire network are becoming cheaper to install and manage. An IT strategy must include plans for the provision of Internet facilities, which are likely to be the most important information retrieval systems in the near future. The multimedia and interactive capabilities of the Internet must also be taken into account.

Remote access to the library

Users will demand access to library facilities just as they are now accessing other services, without the restraints of geography. Many libraries, particularly those in academic institutions, have provided remote access to their online catalogues either through Telnet or more recently through the World Wide Web.

The development of remote access facilities in libraries and other publicly accessible institutions so that users can gain access to information no matter where they reside will be an essential requirement in the future. Thought should be given to the development of facilities that will allow users, especially the disabled and housebound, to access the library network from their own homes.

Public libraries may also need to consider the provision of direct access to the library catalogue and other facilities on the library network from mobile libraries.

Broadband networking
Information superhighway

Telecommunications and cable companies are now working on the main information superhighway infrastructure and most of this will be in place by the millennium. Libraries need to be thinking now about how they can take advantage of this public communications infrastructure both locally and nationally. Opportunities for cooperation with local schools, colleges, libraries and other organizations will multiply in the future as more and more become wired up. Broadband services will blur the distinction between LANs, WANs and the Internet. In the future there will be a seamless and almost immediate transfer of information between desktop, network and Internet.

The development of policies for adopting future facilities in broadband telecommunications and cable systems for the benefit of library users should be included in any IT strategy. Some systems are already in use and gaining in popularity.

ISDN

One option to speed up the transfer of electronic information from one network to another is by using the Integrated Services Digital

Network. Fast connection to external networks, the ability to send voice and fax at the same time over one line or to provide several simultaneous users with Internet access can all be achieved with ISDN. The fast speed of ISDN and the high quality of digital transmission make it ideal for transfer of large graphic files or sound. Video conferencing is another application increasingly being used for more personal communication. Conferencing can include several people and information can be shared on screen at the same time. ISDN is increasingly used for remote security surveillance, providing good-quality video pictures to central points. Cameras can be programmed to transmit only when they have detected a movement in their field of view and thus do not have to remain permanently online. In many large library services with multiple sites holding expensive IT equipment this sort of security can be cost effective. With increasingly valuable investments being made in IT an IT strategy must include provision for security.

ATM and other broadband systems

Although ISDN provides fast transmission of data between networks, even faster transmission speeds will be required for live high-quality video conferencing and other remote multimedia applications. Providing simultaneous access for hundreds of users to remote networks will require far greater bandwidth than ISDN can offer. A number of high-speed technologies are beginning to emerge which will provide a solution to this problem. The most popular is Asynchronous Transfer Mode (ATM), a sophisticated form of packet switching. Packets of data of a fixed size can be routed through optical fibre cable between networks at very high speeds, typically 155 Mb/s, with the potential for increases up to 622 Mb/s in the near future. The data can be voice, text, high-quality audio, fax or full-motion video. ATM will offer a seamless connection between WANs and LANs in the future for the transmission of high bandwidth data such as multimedia. This would permit, for example, the searching of multimedia encyclopedias on CD-ROM from remote sites. The rapid download of large files including software can take place in fractions of a second. ATM facilities can be rented from the major telecommunication companies at differential rates depending upon the speed required.

The rapid growth of multimedia applications on the comparatively slow and narrow bandwidth Internet is an indication of the inexorable move towards fully interactive systems. The next generation of applications will require ATM. The SuperJANET network now operating among academic sites in the UK is the leading example of a high speed optical fibre network, which is being used for a number of actual and experimental projects including distance learning.[4] The London Metropolitan Area Network (MAN), operating within the boundary of the M25, connects 24 universities and colleges with an ATM network operating at between 34 Mb/s and 155 Mb/s.[5] Many other libraries and institutions are likely to be connected to the MAN in the coming year.

Cable companies

The optical fibre cable being laid in large areas of Britain was designed mainly for one way transmission of analogue television into homes. Simultaneous broadcast of many different television channels is possible and telephone traffic can also be sent along a separate channel. The cable companies have been slow to realize the potential for interactive channels on cable but are now looking at the possibility of providing Internet access via cable and at other information transmission possibilities. The cabling of large urban areas has brought cable within reach of many libraries and there may be possibilities to exploit this for future services. Some experimental community information services have been established on cable with the cooperation of local authorities and public libraries. The Gemisis 2000 project in Salford links the University, Salford City Council, health centres, hospitals and other organizations with a high-speed optical fibre network laid by Nynex, the local cable franchisee for Greater Manchester.[6] The cable can provide video, telephone facilities, high bandwidth private circuits up to 34 Mbits and access to SuperJANET.

The library as electronic information provider
Electronic publishing

National, university and public libraries have many unique resources which could be made available to more people than those who presently travel in to libraries to access the physical stock. These resources could be exploited further if they were duplicated in electronic form and made available over networks. This puts the library in the position of being an electronic publisher in its own right rather than merely acting as an intermediary for information produced by others.

There are three main elements in the process:

☐ a digitization programme
☐ a retrieval system
☐ the provision of access

The development of the library's role as an information provider by making electronic information available for downloading directly from the library's own servers, including electronic text, images and shareware both locally and via the Internet, must be considered. For example, many public and university libraries have historical collections that include unique texts and photographs. The retrieval of photographs in particular is often difficult and time consuming from the point of view both of identification of what is required and its physical retrieval from remote storage. Conversion of the photographs to a digitized format together with an automated cataloguing and enquiry facility would enable staff and the public to have speedy access to any individual photograph and to obtain a laser-printed copy whenever one is required. This process is being undertaken in Manchester Central Library where 10,000 images from the Local Studies collection have been digitized. Nationally, many unique resources could be made more widely available through electronic networks. Digitization programmes for uniquely held text and images have to be considered as part of the long-term IT strategy.

World Wide Web and Intranet

Some libraries have already produced their own Web pages. The pages generally consist of guides to the services of the library, useful notes for users, regulations and local information. The pages can be used in a number of ways once they are prepared: they can be put on a Web server on a library's own network as part of an Intranet; alternatively, they can be made available on the Internet either through the library's Web server or by renting space from a commercial Internet provider. As well as straightforward text information, some libraries have produced interesting innovations, particularly on academic library Web sites. American libraries have been particularly innovative with some interesting experimental sites. These include:

□ OPAC access
□ interlibrary loan facilities
□ searchable databases of community information
□ specialist databases such as genealogical records
□ electronic journals
□ library guides and instructions
□ information about local facilities and events.

Some libraries are moving on to the next stage and developing virtual reality and multimedia guides.

All of this work requires time, expertise and a programme for the preparation of electronic material but it is a task which is likely to become more and more necessary in the near future. If such work is to become part of the IT strategy, the staffing and resource implications must be understood and plans prepared.

Once the information is available in electronic form and remote access is provided, libraries can consider moving towards providing 24-hour access to information held on library servers.

Public access computers

Access to information will not be available to a significant number of people in the future if the cost of equipment, software and online charges are too high. Public libraries must provide terminals that are accessible and free or cheap to use to counteract this disadvantage. Universities must provide their students and staff with terminals as a matter of right, as essential tools to access the information and services they will need for their courses. More and more distance learning will be included in courses in the future and remote access will become an everyday activity.

The provision of computers in public libraries for use by the public with a range of popular software such as word-processing, spreadsheets and DTP is becoming more routine. This service has proved very popular in Manchester Public Libraries and has been extended to several sites since its introduction in 1995.

The provision of e-mail and bulletin board facilities would allow members of the library to communicate with staff, with each other and with other users in remote libraries. E-mail is useful for personal, mainly one to one communication: bulletin boards are useful for general discussions, help and advice services and current awareness.

The provision of facilities for open learning and other forms of self-education in public libraries utilizing information technology is an added attraction for library users. Two sites in Manchester Public Libraries provide microcomputers and study desks with all the materials needed and further sites are being considered. Individual interactive courses are available on floppy disks or CD-ROMs which users can follow at their own pace. For those with a home computer, disks and course materials may be borrowed.

Technical design
Technology infrastructure

The above areas for consideration may need to be complemented with others according to the nature of the library or information service and its relationship with its parent body. After considering all the options and deciding on the appropriate way forward there will be the task of utilizing the information to produce a technical infrastructure plan. The main aim of this stage is to produce an outline plan for the future of the library service with the physical components mapped out. This may range from a simple sketch to a detailed plan with an inventory of components depending upon the technical knowledge of the strategy team. Much will depend on whether suppliers have been involved or not at this stage. Complete plans can be produced only after detailed site surveys have been carried out, usually at the implementation stage. The plan will at least indicate the scale of the intended development so that some cost estimates can be made. The main network will be drawn up with terminals and other devices indicated, links to external networks, servers, print and other facilities. A large network may require several stages of implementation and be installed over several years as finance becomes available.

The technology infrastructure of an organization is a combination of the physical infrastructure, the technology architecture, policies, management processes and services.

Physical infrastructure

The strategy will provide a blueprint for the library service consisting of a series of building blocks. These will take the form of statements about the different elements needed to build the vision of the future expressed in the strategy. These building blocks will include details of the intended physical infrastructure, a complex mix of components known as a portfolio of networks, hardware, software, databases, multimedia, information retrieval systems, central files, servers and communications facilities. Most of this will be bought off the shelf from commercial suppliers, although some of the software may be developed in-house if the skills exist. The physical infrastructure also includes the buildings that provide accommodation for IT systems, ancillary equipment, electrical supplies and other physical components.

Technology architecture

The representational plan of these components, together with the information, the processes, the organizational structure and the location of the components, can be described as the technology architecture of the organization. This architecture should ideally be diagrammed to show how the technology infrastructure matches up with the applications and information management. In many organizations this may have developed with few controls. It may never have been accurately mapped and thus exists as a rather mysterious entity.

References

1 'Resources for all', *Library Association record*, March 1997, 128.
2 *COPAC*. **http://copac.ac.uk/copac/**
3 Stafford, Janet, 'The self-service experience at the University of Sunderland', *Its news*, December 1996, 5–16.
4 *What is SuperJANET?*
   http://www.ja.net/SuperJANET/Super...SuperJANET-Intro/Introduction.html
5 London MAN, *Breaking new ground in MAN deployment*.
   http://www.k-net.co.uk/news/net96/lon-man.htm
6 UK National Host GEMISIS 2000, *Description*.
   http://www.salford.ac.uk/docs/depts/eee/nhost/descrip.htm

8 Elements of the strategy – policy and management

The greatest task before civilisation at present is to make machines what they ought to be, the slaves, instead of the masters of men.

Havelock Ellis[1]

Objectives

□ **Develop policies for IT**
□ **Look at the management of future IT systems and support**
□ **Consider the training implications of IT**
□ **Consider improvements to management efficiency**
□ **Consider the budgeting implications of IT**
□ **Look at partnerships with other libraries and organizations**
□ **Consider security.**

Policy and management aims
General aims

The eventual aim is to produce a documented set of policies and procedures for the IT systems in the library service that will enable staff to manage an increasingly complex IT infrastructure as efficiently as possible. An important aim is to devise a structure for the effective management of the current and future IT investment. What is required is a partnership between management and IT specialists that will lead to the achievement of common goals. The aims should be consistent with the overall aims of the library service.

An examination of existing policies should be undertaken to see if there are any policy gaps that need to be filled. Security is often one area where improvements can be made. In the rush to install new equipment and allow users access with minimum restrictions lapses in security are common. These will manifest themselves as problems sooner or later.

Policies
Centralization or decentralization?

The prevailing opinion is that individuals or units should be responsible for managing their own applications on their own personal desktop computers. Some IT support services make agreements with staff about responsibilities and keep an inventory of these to define what can and can not be supported. Other facilities may be centralized, including communications, the choice of hardware and software, security procedures, shared services, upgrading, maintenance, repairs and the ordering of consumables.

However, recent developments in networking and Intranet technology suggest that applications may also become centralized, delivered over the network as and when needed. Information may also become centralized through the centralized control of information formatting, information flows, storage and retrieval. Whatever mix is decided on, there must be a clear definition of roles and responsibilities to prevent confusion and conflict, duplication of effort, inappropriate use of staff resources and a deterioration of systems control.

Openness and access to information

Policies must be devised to determine what controls are to be applied for access to information and the IT systems within the library service. There will need to be varying levels of staff access to information and functions. On a complex network with file servers accessed by a wide variety of users, a system or network manager will be responsible for designing directory structures, will have complete access to all information files and will have authority to grant access to others by providing passwords. Some people, for example cataloguers, will need to have the authority to alter and delete specific records and files on a system. Many other staff and external users may be granted access to read information without changing it. Library users will be able to access a catalogue to check their own borrower records, for instance, but will not have the right to alter the records.

Sensitive and confidential information such as financial management information and personnel files must be strictly controlled with access granted only on a need-to-know basis. Where a library is part of a larger institution this information may be held on corporate systems but made accessible through a network. Controls are needed to ensure that access can be gained only by specific individuals from a limited number of terminals. Logs will need to be maintained on the system of every access so that breaches of security can be followed up if needed.

Accountability

Policies will be needed for assigning responsibility to individuals for a range of functions including: control of files and directories on servers; control of data standards for input to central databases; circulation of management information; responsibility for reporting faults; responsibility for security at different levels; responsibility for equipment, which may be scattered throughout the organization across a number of sites.

New IT systems will inevitably change the existing allocation of responsibilities. New financial and personnel management systems, for example, are often introduced because they provide the opportunity for devolving responsibility down to managers of individual cost centres. Online access to management information allows managers greater control over their areas of responsibility, with less need to call on intermediaries for assistance. At the same time those managers will have a correspondingly greater degree of accountability for their actions.

Replacement policy for library terminals and PCs

A replacement strategy is needed to maintain the effectiveness of existing systems. Equipment can be damaged or stolen. Computer equipment is particularly targeted by thieves because of its high resale value. Security measures should be included in the overall cost of every terminal installed. Each year a proportion of an organization's existing computer equipment may need to be replaced because it is inadequate or obsolete. The cost of upgrading a computer's memory and hard disk may be relatively high and it may be more cost effective to replace the computer rather than upgrade the parts. Older terminals including 'dumb' terminals are generally inadequate for the latest software. These terminals may not be capable, for instance, of being used for CD-ROM searching on a network. Older terminals also create greater maintenance problems. An IT strategy should have some inbuilt flexibility for the gradual replacement of obsolete or inefficient equipment and software. The annual cost of replacement of desktop machines, for example, can be calculated by using a five-year replacement cycle, making an assumption about the initial cost per machine and multiplying by the number of terminals on the network.

Software licensing

Commercial software is copyrighted. A library which allows staff or users to copy software from one computer to another may be liable to prosecution. For this reason only licensed software should be installed. Central purchasing and maintenance of software may be necessary to ensure compliance. Software is freely available on the Internet for downloading but there is always the danger that a virus may be present in an unlicensed program. Rules may be needed to ensure that staff comply with the license conditions for software and do not introduce new programs on to the network without permission.

Management
Staffing for IT

The present staff establishment should be examined to see whether there is a need to formalize posts within the staff structure to meet the need for IT services in the future. In many libraries IT services have been established very quickly, often by staff seconded from other work who may not have become fully integrated into the existing structure. There is a need to make provision for IT maintenance, management and development. Posts may need to be created to meet the needs of the service in the future. The impact of IT on some traditional jobs in the library such as cataloguing and acquisitions may lead to the creation of new, more integrated units.

The creation of new posts needed for the maintenance and development of electronic systems may include:

☐ network managers and systems staff
☐ software specialists and programmers
☐ maintenance and support staff
☐ database staff
☐ information managers and Internet/Intranet staff.

The larger the library service the greater the need will be for specialist staff. The proportion of staff devoted to IT tasks will continue to grow as IT becomes more pervasive.

IT support services

There are many different tasks to be undertaken by an IT support service. Some or all may be undertaken centrally by an IT unit or tasks may be delegated to a variety of staff within the library service. A library is likely to have a wide range of IT systems for both staff and users which requires different task groups. Some of the tasks of IT support are listed below:

Providing services to users
☐ network management
☐ maintenance of hardware
☐ routine operations on larger systems
☐ providing communications facilities
☐ quality control.

Database management
☐ database maintenance
☐ access control
☐ data integrity and standards
☐ security etc.

Infrastructure development
☐ providing facilities across the library service
☐ network extension and rationalization
☐ organizing pilot studies for new implementations.

Systems development
☐ system design
☐ software development on larger systems.

Advice centre
☐ telephone and personal support for existing applications software
☐ providing advice on new applications
☐ carrying out feasibility studies for users.

Central purchase and brokerage
☐ software packages
☐ external services
☐ equipment purchases etc.

Planning
☐ new systems
☐ monitoring new technical developments
☐ technology forecasting etc.

The assignment of responsibilities for all of these areas must be carefully worked out. Policies may be required for many of the functions to avoid any confusion and duplication of effort. A good deal of valuable staff time can be wasted in organizations when highly paid staff spend their time trying to sort out minor technical problems with software or hardware which should be done by IT staff.

In larger organizations a detailed staff structure will be required for IT support services, covering all the functions listed.

IT manager

The IT function in any organization will need to be properly managed. There should be an individual with overall responsibility for the implementation of the IT strategy and its continued maintenance and development. The importance of IT in most organizations is recognized now by a post at senior management level. An IT manager will often have responsibility for a large operating budget, several staff and more importantly for operational functions within the organization that are vital for the day-to-day running of the library's services. With IT permeating every area of an organization's work, the responsibility is too great to be delegated to a post merely at operational or middle management level. Another reason for placing the IT manager at a senior level is to enable authority to be centralized at the top of the organization. The need to establish and enforce standards for data input and maintenance, for open systems and common applications to permit efficient communication across the organization, means that authority has to come from senior management. Failure to provide this authority will inevitably lead to a lack of control, with individuals or units going their own way and implementing a mixture of systems that are difficult to support and integrate.

Many library services have IT officers who are technicians whose role has been to maintain equipment on standalone systems or small networks. The penetration of IT into every aspect of the organization and the growth of complex networks which have become their operational backbones demands a more strategic and managerial role. The IT function is ceasing to be simply another support service in the library service but is becoming one of the main management challenges and its importance will continue to grow in the future in parallel with the growth of complex communication networks. Senior managers in future will need to be highly computer literate rather than depending upon and deferring to junior colleagues for advice and guidance. The role of IT manager will thus become increasingly concerned with strategic management of IT rather than just technical support.

IT steering group

IT developments in many organizations are often controlled, usually rather loosely, by some form of working party, strategy group, steering committee or coordinating body. This may be led by a member of senior management and is designed to ensure some form of management involvement in the IT process. It is also designed to provide different parts of the organization with a say in IT policies and allows for better communication throughout the organization. By bringing together different levels of knowledge and attitudes towards IT, the steering group can serve to change views and to motivate users and non-users. It can provide people with an opportunity to learn more about IT so they can disseminate awareness of IT systems throughout the organization.

There is often a culture gap in many organizations in which the IT function has become a specialty delegated to a small group that has developed its own sub-culture. Communication between the specialists in this group and other staff is often limited. The steering group can be useful in bringing together specialists and non-specialists in a way that forces them to communicate together.

People are given an opportunity to put forward ideas for their own areas of responsibility and know that they are feeding into the main strategy of the organization.

Other working parties may also be established to deal with technical issues and the resolution of operational problems thrown up by new systems. These problems should be dealt with separately, not by a management group. The introduction of a new library circulation system, for example, will require work to be done on configuration, testing, procedures and operational training.

The main purpose of the IT steering group should be to ensure that the strategic objectives of the IT strategy are carried out effectively. It will be the main forum for initial debate of the IT strategy when it has been drafted. The group should have sufficient responsibility and influence to ensure that the IT strategy has the support of the library management and that the resources for it will be taken out of competition with other demands. The group should provide an effective consensus for the adoption of the IT strategy.

IT skills for library staff
Training and staff development

The first consideration is the provision of training in basic IT skills and general software such as word-processing to increase staff efficiency. All library staff need to have such skills. Front-line staff will need to be trained not only in the use of computerized issue and discharge systems and catalogue querying but in CD-ROM searching, Windows-based software, the Internet, database interrogation and the use of other systems.

It is important to provide continuous training for staff in order to improve upon basic IT skills so that new IT developments can be introduced with a minimum of fuss. Improvements in services to users will occur only if staff are trained effectively. Staff will also need to be trained to help library users make the most of IT equipment in the library service, including the use of software packages and information retrieval systems. Staff must feel confident that they can deal with day-to-day problems raised by users of IT systems in the library. The improvement of IT skills and the growing knowledge about IT among staff should generate further ideas for IT developments in the library service.

Plans need to be formulated to prepare staff for new services that may be introduced in the years ahead. Increasing staff awareness of new technology and systems such as multimedia and the Internet will help to pave the way for their smooth introduction.

IT training is likely to absorb a greater proportion of the training budget in future and the size of training budgets may need to be considered. IT training can be expensive and needs to be looked at on a more cooperative basis. The possibilities of sharing training with other local organizations should be investigated.

Job descriptions

Training is essential but so also is the need to review job descriptions and person specifications for many posts in the library service. The growing dependence of libraries on IT and the need for most staff to have IT skills means that IT inevitably has an effect upon the wider issues of staff management. Training in IT skills is obviously important but managers will be looking for skills in the marketplace to reduce the overhead of expensive training in IT. Increasingly, recruitment will focus on IT skills as one component in a range of skills needed in modern and changing library services. These skills will be increasingly incorporated into job descriptions and person specifications.

Improving management efficiency
Management skills

Managerial staff are making increasing use of word-processing, spreadsheets, e-mail and file transfer software over internal and external networks. Managers should not depend upon other staff carrying out this work on their behalf but for greater efficiency should be able to undertake it themselves. Failure to acquire the skills needed for these tasks will limit an individual's ability to plug into the existing organizational culture. The ability to create, retrieve, forward and re-use text on a desktop computer is becoming a basic skill for managers.

Text management

Management efficiency can be significantly improved by making full use of desktop computer facilities for the creation, storage and transmission of documents. The standardization of text input so that text can be distributed on the network must be acknowledged and practised by managers and other staff. Documents can then be stored on a central network server for access by managers from their own terminals.

An attempt should be made to integrate the flow of text through word-processing, DTP and other processes so that several products can be produced from one body of text. Text need be created only once electronically and it can then be available for cutting and pasting into many different documents.

Management information

The production of management information such as detailed performance statistics using spreadsheets has become commonplace. The collection and collation of library statistics and their circulation to managers is usually done centrally at monthly or quarterly intervals. The storage of such management information on a network server for retrieval by managers can help to improve efficiency. Information can be retrieved when required, added to new work and subjected to a variety of changes to model future trends. The information can be extracted for use in reports or circulated with more detailed commentary to other staff. Accessibility is the main consideration.

Information retrieval

Managers need access to external as well as internal information resources. The provision of desktop retrieval facilities, especially Internet access, will be a necessary requirement in the near future. The wealth of background information on the Internet will allow a manager to quickly find information, download it and incorporate it into working documents without moving from the desktop.

Communication

Communication is one of the most important activities of a manager. Electronic communication systems have advanced greatly in recent years. The use of e-mail, fax software and the transfer of documents, images and software from one organization to another has increased dramatically. The provision of such facilities for managers and other staff is becoming more important and must be taken into account in any strategy. A communications strategy should form part of the overall IT strategy.

Group working

Network communication using groupware has proved to be useful for groups of people working on projects who may be scattered in an organization but need to communicate frequently. People can work on the same documents, send messages, make changes and suggestions or communicate new ideas at any time without having to meet physically. Electronic diaries can provide a quick means for arranging meetings and scheduling work. Providing the facilities for effective group working may be an important consideration for the strategy.

Marketing

The use of IT to extend and improve the marketing and publicity of library services should be investigated. By making full use of DTP and other facilities a good deal of publicity material can be created in-house. Communications software can be used to distribute information for publicity purposes. Statistical information can be collected from library systems and used to assess demand for market planning. The Internet offers a relatively cheap method of marketing services to users and potential users. Marketing will be part of the overall management strategy of any library service and the IT strategy should make provision for it.

Budgeting for IT
Capital costs

The large capital outlay needed for extensive IT developments across a library service may be a major obstacle to implementation. Public sector organizations cannot raise external finance in the way that a commercial company can by producing a business plan with details of how the new technology will generate increased profits to pay for the investment. Capital funding in most libraries is dependent upon the parent or funding body. Plans need to be outlined well in advance to fit in with the normal budget cycles. There are usually many more competing claims upon the capital money available each year than can be satisfied so it is important to prepare capital bids for IT carefully and to win senior management support at an early stage.

Systems suppliers usually expect to be paid in stages over a number of years as the project they are introducing is rolled out. In this way capital expenditure can be managed more easily and revenue budgets may be used partly to pay for IT projects. Negotiations with suppliers may allow for the bulk purchase at a discount of terminals or other pieces of equipment from third-party suppliers. Much equipment now used by proprietary library systems is standard and better discounts from authorized suppliers may be available to large organizations such as local authorities.

There are many separate costs associated with the introduction of new IT systems. There are the straightforward and easily quantifiable costs of the new hardware, software and network cabling. Systems configuration may be an additional cost. Installation of a large system and its peripherals may be less easy to cost until detailed site surveys have been carried out by a contractor.

Accommodation may be needed for new equipment or extra space may need to be found within existing rooms. This may cause the displacement of other functions which must then be relocated. New furniture, which may be designed to meet strict health and safety standards, may be needed.

Unless leasing is used, most capital costs will be one-off costs and can be seen as a strategic investment for the future.

Leasing

Leasing deals may be available to allow library services to lease standard equipment in part or in whole from specialized financial or computer leasing companies. These will allow payments to be made over several years from revenue budgets. In some cases the payments are deferred so that a period of free running is allowed. This can obviously have a big impact on the revenue budget when payments fall due but it does help to spread the cost of large capital projects.

Leasing restrictions may exist. In some cases software is not leasable. Equipment is often leasable only if it is free standing and can be taken away if necessary. Installation work such as cabling may not be leasable because it is fixed in position and suitable only for the site in which it was installed.

Revenue or ownership costs

Whether IT systems are financed through capital expenditure or leasing they will have an effect upon revenue budgets. Revenue costs are just as important as capital costs in assessing the overall benefits to be gained from IT investments. Too many organizations make the mistake of underestimating the revenue consequences of capital expenditure when embarking on large-scale capital projects. There are many running costs associated with IT systems which will add to the general overheads of the library service, even without any revenue consequences from capital financing. These must be budgeted for as part of the strategy.

Increased overheads will include:

☐ electricity consumption
☐ telecommunications costs
☐ consumables
☐ training costs
☐ insurance
☐ security
☐ maintenance.

Electricity consumption can rise dramatically when a network with dozens of terminals and printers is installed. Networking brings its own costs which may include the cost of any rented dedicated telecommunication lines and ISDN rental and call charges.

It can be difficult to estimate the true cost of consumables because these are often aggregated within general budgets. Consumables can be expensive and must be properly budgeted for. Paradoxically, IT systems tend to increase the use of paper in the short-term partly because many more people have access to printers than they ever had to typewriters. Printing is not cheap: paper costs have risen sharply in recent years and toner cartridges for laser printers can cost from £50 to £100.

Training has both direct costs in the form of course fees, equipment or venue hire and many hidden costs such as staff time away from service points or preparation time which should be accounted for. Other indirect costs are the management time involved in planning, assessing and implementing new systems and reviewing their success.

Security for expensive, portable and desirable computers is essential and this may involve a range of measures to protect the investments made. Insurance, security plates to physically tie down desktop computers, CCTV cameras for vulnerable areas, disk drive locks and other devices may be needed.

Annual maintenance should be costed as a percentage of the capital cost of hardware. This may be between 10% and 20% of the capital cost. There may need to be backup for certain operational equipment in case of breakdown.

Revenue budgets may need to be adjusted to take into account the increased costs of IT provision. Wherever possible, budgets should be disaggregated into cost centres to make this process easier. It is obvious that revenue costs will increase in proportion to the amount of equipment being added and most libraries will be faced with mounting revenue costs for IT in the future. This fact should be spelled out clearly in the strategy.

Partnerships
Strategic alliances

Libraries will need to develop partnerships with other libraries, both public and academic, with other organizations including private companies, in the UK and abroad, to fund further IT developments and applications. This kind of cooperation is common in the United States where a number of experiments are being carried out on public access Internet projects sponsored by major companies.

Networking is a cooperative process and will become increasingly important by the millennium. Libraries will no longer be isolated from each other or from their users. Networks will connect libraries together in a direct way, allowing them to share resources more effectively for the benefit of everyone. Universal access will become increasingly possible.

Another reason for forming cooperative partnerships is to develop strategic alliances which can influence future developments. Larger groupings are more likely to influence government policy and public opinion. Libraries are too often unseen and unheard, unacknowledged and underestimated. Developing cooperative IT strategies would enable them to create more of an impact.

Other libraries

The development of cooperative partnerships with other library services whether locally, nationally or internationally, with a view to joint development and exploitation of electronic networking, will become increasingly common. Joint projects with neighbouring library services for the mutual benefit of library users in the local area is the most likely development. The division of some of the old county councils into unitary authorities has created some small public library services with few resources to carry out their functions effectively. Networking between such services could provide operating efficiencies and a wider access to information for the public.

Consideration should be given to electronic networking between public and academic libraries with the possibility of all linking in to the same broadband networks in the future. This would ensure that scarce resources are shared more effectively.

The formation of partnerships with other European libraries is becoming more common. Through its 4th Framework Telematics Programme the EU has recognized the role libraries can play in the development of IT systems by making money available for innovative electronic projects in libraries. Cooperation with libraries from other countries will become increasingly common. The Internet is already helping to break down the geographical boundaries between libraries. Worldwide access to the catalogues of other libraries is now possible through the World Wide Web. Librarians are already developing links with their colleagues in other countries through e-mail and newsgroups, cooperating at an informal level by giving advice and information. This process could be extended further into cooperation in the development of Internet and World Wide Web projects which can be carried out remotely.

Security
Physical security

With more and more valuable IT equipment being installed in libraries precautions must be taken to protect it. Insurance for computers is becoming increasingly costly, with excess claim limits often greater than the cost of even a top-of-the-range microcomputer. Security arrangements for existing systems should be reviewed and, where appropriate and practicable, improved.

Buildings housing IT equipment should be secure. Public buildings that are staffed during the day and evening may not be such a problem, providing there is adequate supervision of the IT equipment. When the buildings are closed there is the threat of break-ins and burglaries. Existing alarm systems may need to be assessed to see if they are adequate. Extra security may be needed such as grilles or bars on vulnerable entry points. CCTV and security patrols may need to be considered if a lot of new equipment is installed in a high-risk site.

Apart from securing buildings, other physical measures may need to be adopted such as the use of security plates and cables on desktop computers, disk drive locks and lockable storage cabinets for equipment or supplies to protect against opportunist thieves, vandals and general accidents. Although different measures will be needed for different circumstances, a general policy of adding in a security cost element for every machine purchased will be necessary.

Protecting access and confidentiality

Networks are vulnerable to malicious intruders who may hack into systems as a challenge, to obtain confidential information or to cause deliberate damage. Systems must be protected from unauthorized use. The number of people allowed access to sensitive information should be strictly controlled. Staff should be registered and requested to sign an agreement which states the extent of their access rights. Systems access should require user identification and passwords. Passwords should be allocated to individuals and kept secret. Penalties need to be applied to staff who fail to ensure adequate security.

Public terminals should be set up in a way that prevents access to system files and directories. If popular software packages are used these may need to have functions disabled to prevent users from gaining access to the operating system. The use of Internet software and CD-ROM software on networks is particularly problematic and extra security software may need to be installed to prevent users hacking into other parts of the network through standard software.

Remote access facilities carry their own dangers. Secure firewalls will need to be established before remote users are allowed to access the internal network.

Security is an overhead cost which must be allowed for in the strategy. Breaches of security are often the result of staff carelessness or naïvety when passwords or access procedures are revealed to outsiders. All staff must be aware that security is a shared responsibility.

Viruses

Users should not be able to put their own floppy disks into public terminals, nor should they be allowed to upload files on to a system. Virus-checking software should be running on a network so that automatic checks are carried out whenever a terminal is logged in. The virus software will need to be kept up to date to deal with any new viruses that appear. If users are to be allowed to use their own disks these should be checked automatically for viruses before use.

Security policies

All the above measures for security need to be incorporated as policies in an IT strategy. Many organizations have comprehensive policy documents relating to IT security. Security strategies are often produced in great detail. Breaches of security may be regarded as serious enough for disciplinary action to be taken, with staff dismissal the ultimate penalty. With libraries becoming more dependent upon networked systems for their day-to-day running, a serious breach of security could jeopardize the whole operation. The cost of recovery might be very high. Services must be protected from disruption and this means applying limits to access, defining responsibilities clearly and taking decisive action on breaches of security.

Risk management

Libraries are becoming dependent upon IT for many of their critical operations and thought must be given to protecting the IT investments. Problems can arise in many ways. One of the main problems is the possibility of power failure. Systems must be able to recover without undue delay or loss of data.

Risks can be reduced if they are managed by having policies for the following:

☐ power failure
☐ fire
☐ theft
☐ frequent and secure backing up of data
☐ extended equipment warranty
☐ insurance
☐ maintenance contracts
☐ spares holding
☐ replacement.

Policy and management statements

When all the appropriate areas have been considered a list of policy statements should be agreed and produced as part of an IT strategy document. The policies will be made available for all staff to see so that the strategy is understood. The policies will represent commitments by senior management to staff and users so they must be fair, accurate and guaranteed.

References

1   Ellis, Havelock, *Little essay of love and virtue*, Ch 7, 1922.

9 Evaluation and implementation

Even the best plan degenerates into work.

Anon

Objectives

- □ Evaluate strategy plans before detailed implementation
- □ Develop implementation plans
- □ Consider the problems of implementing large systems
- □ Look at alternatives for financing IT development
- □ Plan staffing for implementation
- □ Produce specifications for tender
- □ Plan for installation and testing
- □ Plan staff training
- □ Consider risks.

Evaluation of the strategy
Evaluation stages

Evaluation of the strategy will take place at a number of stages. The outline strategy will need to be evaluated before implementation is agreed. Evaluation will also take place during and after implementation at the monitoring and review stages. Senior management must be confident that the IT strategy fulfils the needs of the library or information service for the next few years and that all the important areas for development of the service have been taken into account. Only then can the strategy be adopted and endorsed.

Factors affecting the adoption of an IT strategy

The external as well as the internal demands of the library service should have been considered including those of suppliers, users and related organizations. Looking at improvements to services rather than looking for cost reductions is likely to improve the chances of an IT strategy being successful. IT systems rarely reduce overall costs but can lead to significant improvements in service through greater efficiency and effectiveness.

Other factors that will play a significant role in the evaluation of an IT strategy include:

☐ the cost of using IT systems once they have been introduced
☐ the number and range of applications the library can cope with
☐ the skills and expertise available to develop IT systems
☐ external pressures on the library service to improve its services or performance
☐ the ability of management to understand IT and make sound judgements about its introduction.

Integration

A strategy should take account of the needs of the whole library service rather than allowing one part to gain an advantage over another because of rivalry between departments or individuals. The benefits must be shared across the whole of the library service. Confining the benefits to one department could create a spurious importance leading to an imbalance of resources within the organization which would ultimately be to everyone's disadvantage. The IT strategy should be used as an opportunity to integrate systems rather than to allow them to diverge from each other.

Piloting new IT projects

It may be possible to introduce new IT systems as pilot projects so that problems can be assessed in a controlled way and improvements made before the systems are rolled out across the library service. Finding an IT application that will be an early success, one that can be quickly implemented and will bring benefits in a short time will enhance the credibility of the IT strategy. This may be a useful starting point for evaluating the impact of the strategy.

Assessing the advantages of the IT strategy

Where IT systems have already been introduced the way in which they operate should be looked at carefully to see if any further benefits can be gained. It is often possible to utilize IT systems in new ways as expertise grows and ideas are generated. There can be useful spin-offs from systems which become apparent only after the system has been working for some time. In Manchester, a graphics package which came free with a database program proved so easy to use that it became the first software package for training staff, providing a useful and practical introduction to computers. The program allowed staff to produce notices, leaflets and posters for the library within minutes rather than wait for weeks to have them printed.

☐ Will the IT strategy lead to better use of existing IT facilities?
☐ Will the IT strategy improve quality?

Among the benefits IT can bring is being at the cutting edge of developments. A reputation for innovation can attract the bright, the adventurous and the entrepreneurial. Universities compete for students and for the better qualified staff who can in turn attract research funds and projects which add to the general forward-looking image. The further ahead the library service becomes the more likely it is to pick up on opportunities its competitors would miss.

☐ Will the IT strategy move the library service forward?
☐ Will the IT strategy enhance the reputation of the library service?

IT can be useful in developing strategic alliances with other organizations which produce an advantage based on cooperation and the sharing of knowledge and expertise. The EU has sponsored several research projects in recent years under the electronic libraries programme. Such projects provide models and practical benefits for other libraries and also act as catalysts in the development of expertise in the cooperating organizations, so that the general level of IT knowledge increases and provides a firm foundation for further developments.

☐ Does the IT strategy include proposals for cooperative projects?

Many new services have been developed with IT systems. Academic and public library users are increasingly able to access information via the Internet through terminals provided as part of the general range of services. Access to databases of local information is improving the search for useful community information. Freely available word-processing facilities for library users have been introduced in many places. The tedious process of searching for information in newspapers and journals has been substantially improved by the introduction of networked CD-ROMs. E-mail facilities are gradually being provided to enable users to communicate with each other and with those hidden behind the institutional façades that provide the services. These improvements in the delivery of information to users have consequent effects upon the efficiency of individuals to deal with the management of their own work, providing them with advantages which cannot be quantifiably measured but that add significantly to their perception of the quality of the service.

☐ Will the IT strategy introduce new services?
☐ Will the IT strategy directly benefit users?
☐ Will the IT strategy produce measurable improvements in efficiency?
☐ Will the IT strategy provide better access to information?

IT can have an impact at every level, changing the nature of the whole organization, acting upon the different functions within the library service and affecting the individuals who run and use it. Libraries are gradually moving away from the closed, intimidating archival storehouse model of tradition towards that of an open service-based operation providing quick, easy and anonymous access to information that can be taken away in convenient personalized packages.

☐ Will the IT strategy change the way the library service operates?
☐ Will the IT strategy provide a better image of the service?

Within the library service IT may help to change the internal balance of power between functions by releasing resources from collection-based activities such as cataloguing, acquisitions and stock control towards service and information provision.

☐ Will the IT strategy release resources in the library service?

Through the use of desktop computers individual members of staff can be given more power to communicate with each other, to gather information more easily, to develop their own current awareness systems, to prepare their own word-processed reports and to do many other tasks themselves which in the past required a support services structure with specialist staff. The simple act of producing a letter on a word-processor in five minutes compared with the complex negotiation with a central typing pool, drafting, proofreading and correcting over several hours, if not days, is an example of how cost and time savings can be made. With the use of computer faxing or e-mail even more time can be saved on correspondence and thus spent on other work.

☐ Will the IT strategy improve communications?
☐ Will the IT strategy improve staff efficiency?
☐ Will the IT strategy save time?

Implementation as part of strategy
Outline of the implementation process

This chapter is not intended to cover in detail the implementation of an IT system. What is given here is a general outline of the implementation process and some of the factors that are common to IT projects such as producing specifications for tender. There are several books such as the one by Price which give detailed guidance on managing the implementation of computer systems.[1] Different IT projects will require detailed implementation plans which may be quite different in sequences and procedures. A given IT strategy may have proposals for several different projects with varying degrees of priority. A timetable for implementation will be needed. Where projects are not interdependent they may be implemented in parallel, whereas others may be implemented only in a planned sequence; a network may need to be established or improved, for example, before a particular service can be introduced.

Is implementation part of developing a strategy?

An IT strategy needs to include plans for implementation. That is, the strategy must take into account the problems to be overcome in implementing the recommended IT proposals. Implementation itself is a process that comes after the IT strategy has been accepted and financed. In that sense the implementation is a separate phase from the IT strategy process. On the other hand, once an IT strategy has been implemented the performance of the IT systems must be monitored and the strategy reviewed in the light of experience.

This reinforces the view that strategy is a continuous process rather than a once for all exercise. The results of implementing the short-term proposals will be assessed and the details fed into the next phase of the strategy. The IT strategy is thus a dynamic model rather than a static one. The strategy should be updated on a regular basis, probably annually to fit in with the updating of the annual service plans and budget cycles common to most organizations.

Implementation planning

Implementation requirements

Once the details of the IT strategy have been approved the strategy must be implemented. This requires:

☐ the right level of resourcing
☐ sensible allocation of the resources
☐ the implementation of an appropriate structure to deal with the new strategy
☐ the motivation of staff to achieve the necessary changes.

Stages

There are a number of distinct stages in the implementation of an IT strategy. These can be applied to large or small projects but there is obviously much more involved in the introduction of a circulation system for a library service or building a library service network than, say, equipping a graphics unit with new DTP facilities.

Staff awareness

Implementation should include plans for ensuring that all staff in the library service are aware of and understand the IT strategy. This will include the circulation of any public strategy documents and may include workshops and awareness sessions to deal with any questions and fears about the strategy. The support of senior management will be demonstrated by the statements and actions of the senior management team.

Prioritizing

The IT strategy should eventually include a list of desirable IT systems that the library service wishes to install. Each of these systems will require a separate project. If there are many projects some degree of priority will need to be assigned to them to produce a practical implementation plan. The library service may not be able to cope with the upheaval and confusion of installing a large number of new systems all at once. Extensive training may be needed for staff. There will inevitably be some restructuring to make allowances for the management and maintenance of new IT systems and the disestablishment of posts associated with older processes now made obsolete.

Choosing priorities may not be an easy task. This is the task of the IT strategy steering group or the senior management team. The process will include assessments for each project of:

☐ the risks of implementing or not implementing
☐ the estimated costs, including staff time
☐ the technical feasibility and the expertise available
☐ the timescale
☐ the benefits expected from the implementation.

The projects need to be ranked in priority order for implementation. Most, but not all, projects will require resources, particularly staff time, to implement them. An assessment must be made of what resources are needed, when they will be needed and where they can be found. The constraints upon library budgets in recent years has meant that many developments have had to be carried out with existing resources. The implementation of new IT systems may therefore have to take priority over other operations. The possible disruptive effects of this, especially upon services to users, must be carefully assessed and justified.

There are a number of ways of prioritizing projects, such as:

☐ putting projects into high (essential), medium (desirable) and low (possible) categories
☐ scoring each project against a list of priorities for the library service
☐ ranking from fundamental (backbone) to peripheral (requiring an infrastructure first)
☐ short timescale to long timescale
☐ comparing those showing quickest return on investment to those with longer-term benefit

There are advantages in ensuring that priority is given to projects which will show a rapid return on their investment, ones from which staff can see benefits quickly.

Project plans

Project management plans for each of these priorities must be drawn up. The main elements in such plans are:

☐ agreeing project aims and scope
☐ assessing resources
☐ assigning a team
☐ setting out a timetable with milestones for achievement
☐ undertaking any necessary research and training
☐ examining constraints and problems
☐ planning each action stage
☐ establishing procedures for monitoring and review.

Staff training and responsibilities

Programmes for awareness and training of other staff may need to be devised and carried out. These may be workshops, seminars or system training, depending on the project. Manuals and guidelines in using the new systems may need to be produced if they are not included in the supplier's package. In most cases, local use of a new system will demand local guidelines.

For complex new systems the guidelines will be extensive and may include:

- □ the responsibilities of individuals
- □ how information on the system is to be added, deleted and kept up to date
- □ rules for organizing information on the system
- □ codes of conduct and penalties for abuse
- □ legal requirements for data protection
- □ security procedures.

Change management

In many cases the new systems, particularly large, complex systems, will have a fundamental effect upon working practices, roles and relationships within the library service and preparations must be made for this. Some jobs may become redundant as a result of the introduction of a new system and new ones may need to be created. This implies that staff restructuring may be necessary. These changes must be managed effectively if full benefits are to be achieved from the new systems. A programme of change management may be needed.

Implementing large systems
In-house versus outside contractor

One of the main decisions is whether to do the work within the organization or to contract it to outsiders. It might be cheaper to do the work in-house if there are staff available with the right expertise. More control might then be exercised over the system design. But the absence of a formal specification may lead to looser control and a fall in standards. Few library services have the degree of expertise needed to produce the sophisticated systems demanded by users. Many users are computer-literate nowadays and are used to using sophisticated interfaces such as Windows. To develop a sophisticated system in-house would require a considerable degree of programming expertise and commitment and could take years of effort. Even if the expertise was there it might not be possible to devote the necessary staff to a long, complicated project.

Library systems

In the case of a large project such as a new library circulation system it is more likely that a package will be bought in from a recognized and experienced supplier of which there are a number in the marketplace. Such suppliers will do all the work in installing the system, testing it and maintaining it. In the past some libraries programmed their own systems, usually with help from corporate IT units which were heavily oriented towards mainframe systems and had to derive maximum use from these expensive installations. There was an inevitable bias towards fitting the design to an existing computer rather than finding the best solution to the needs of the library service. Some library services still have such systems but the trend is to move towards supplier systems. These modern library systems have been developed over many years and have been well tested in the marketplace. The networked system is now the preferred model and it is unlikely that a library service would want to have a system that is not integrated with its network development plans.

Network evolution

Most libraries have suppliers' proprietary systems based on minicomputers which are thus independent of corporate facilities. These systems were usually designed to allow remote sites to connect into a central system centre through a wide area network using leased lines. On the central site a local area network was sometimes established with terminals connected for the circulation system. Other multipurpose terminals could be then be added to the LAN, providing access to CD-ROMs and internal databases as well as the main catalogue. This tended to isolate the library system from corporate developments.

Establishing links to corporate systems has become more advantageous with the development of online financial and personnel management systems. Many corporate broadband networks have been established and more recently Intranets have begun to appear, linking together different corporate departments. Libraries have realized that they cannot remain isolated from other network developments. As networks become more extensive there is a need to involve more people from different parts of the parent organization in making decisions about interconnections.

Replacing a system
Upgrading

At some point there will be the need to replace an older computer system with a more up to date one. This may be may be undertaken for a number of reasons:

☐ the hardware showing its age
☐ reliability problems
☐ maintenance costs rising as the equipment becomes obsolete
☐ difficulty in obtaining spare parts
☐ changes to the original system so that it no longer works as an efficient entity
☐ conflicts causing frequent problems, even breakdowns
☐ support staff leaving
☐ difficulties in finding new staff who know about or are interested in an older system
☐ the system becoming overloaded by a growing database beyond its specification
☐ the demands of users for faster response times or for more up-to-date interfaces.

Choosing the right time to replace a system is important. This must be well before the older system has reached a point where breakdown is likely. An IT strategy should include at least an outline plan for the retirement of a system and a realistic assessment of its likely lifespan.

System migration

Moving from one supplier's system to that of another may be the only way to obtain all the facilities needed in a new system. This presents different problems from the upgrading process. Although the data can usually be transferred unaltered, both hardware and software may need to be changed and the existing network upgraded as well. There are many management problems involved with such a radical change. More detailed justification and costing will be necessary for the new system. The EU procurement regulations will need to be considered for an expensive project of this sort. Tendering will be necessary and detailed specifications will need to be drawn up. The work needed to undertake this must be carefully considered.

Cooperative agreements

Some library services in local areas have formed cooperative groups to run systems. Some academic libraries have cooperated by using the same supplier's system so that records can be shared and interfaces developed to a standard specification. Public libraries in some neighbouring authorities have formed groups to run their services from a single combined database to which their individual networks can connect. Such cooperative projects may become more common in future as networks develop further. Software that is evolving for Internet use may actually render proprietary software from suppliers obsolete. Until this happens local cooperative schemes should be considered with neighbouring libraries to see if there can be any savings from joint development or purchase of systems. Some suppliers now offer facilities management packages and will undertake to maintain several systems run from their own site. The library networks are thus connected to remote system centres on suppliers' premises and can benefit from shared resources.

Outsourcing

With the increasing complexity of IT systems and networks and the rapid changes in hardware and software which are making systems obsolete within shorter and shorter timescales, many organizations are looking at outsourcing their IT requirements. This may be anything from contracting for external support to leasing whole systems from suppliers. Leased systems of this sort may even be remotely located on supplier premises and accessed by virtual networks. The advantages of this kind of contract are that systems can be changed without the need for large capital investment, which many organizations, particularly in the public sector, find difficult to finance. The annual costs may be higher for such contracts but financing out of revenue may be easier for some organizations than capital expenditure. The disadvantages are those associated with dealing with problems remotely and the need to find a continual stream of revenue funding to maintain the contract. The financial integrity and stability of the supplier is obviously an important consideration in deciding to outsource a system. The contract specification will be crucial in ensuring that key operations function effectively and there are adequate safeguards to prevent breakdowns in any services being operated.

Some library suppliers are now offering this kind of service and it should be considered seriously in any strategy. Commercial organizations are using outsourcing in a big way and it is growing in popularity, although it is not without its critics. Currie describes some of the problems.[2] It has been less popular with public sector organizations which have difficulties in committing large sections of their revenue budgets to pay for outsourcing.

Staffing for implementation
The project team

Any large-scale implementation of IT systems and networks requires a good deal of input from the library side as well as the supplier side. This is normally achieved by establishing a project team. The composition of the team is crucial to the successful implementation of the project. To work effectively the team needs to be free from departmental interference, operating as an independent unit reporting either to a steering committee or direct to the senior management team. One of the main difficulties faced by such teams can be the pull of internal politics within the organization. One example of this is a power struggle for control of the project between the traditional computer department and the end users of a system. Technical experts, who may be keen to satisfy their desire for yet bigger and more complex computer systems for their own prestige and advancement need to be balanced by end users who are more interested in obtaining a workable, practical system that is simple enough to use and robust enough to rely on for day-to-day operations. Staff chosen for the project should, as far as possible, be taken away from their normal work for the timescale of the implementation to allow them sufficient time to devote to the project. Some projects will require complete dedication to the implementation.

There are many advantages in adopting this approach. More staff will have the opportunity to learn in detail about the system, they will have a greater understanding of its limitations and its advantages, and they will have the opportunity to influence the way in which it is implemented within the library service. Their personal input to the project is more likely to make them advocates for the system when it comes into operation and other staff become users. Some may later form the nucleus of the support team for the operational system.

The project manager

A project manager or leader will have the task of implementing new IT projects to meet the functions, timescale and financial aims defined by senior management. The role of the project manager is to lead the project team, which will be responsible for negotiating with the suppliers and overseeing installation.

Team building and training

The project team may need initial training to manage the project effectively. Project definition workshops are sometimes used to ensure that all members of the team are aware of the main objectives and their roles on the project. These normally follow a well defined pattern, including:

☐ the appointment of a project sponsor, usually a senior manager
☐ the appointment of a project manager and team
☐ the production of a mission statement
☐ listing the objectives
☐ listing changes needed to meet the objectives
☐ listing assumptions or uncertainties and the potential risks arising from them.

A project review board led by the project sponsor will have regular meetings to discuss progress. Complex projects can take several weeks or months to plan in detail.

Management training may be needed to give members project management skills. Once a supplier has been chosen the project team will need to become familiar with the supplier's systems or products in detail. This is best done on the job with supplier's staff and should form part of any contract with the supplier.

Team requirements

A project team may require a range of skills. These may not be required all at the same time and different people will be needed at different stages to advise on areas that require special expertise. Legal advice may be needed, for example, in drawing up the conditions in a contract or in interpreting a supplier's contract.

Financial expertise may be needed in monitoring or analysing the finances of a project. Large systems and complex networks can cost hundreds of thousands, or even millions of pounds, so it is essential that expenditure is properly accounted for. Suppliers may offer a variety of alternative payment deals to overcome some of the financial obstacles libraries would face with large capital projects. The implications of these need to be properly understood before decisions are made.

Administrators who are at home with procedures and rules are needed to ensure that systems are kept under control and their use is properly organized, documented and monitored. Sophisticated systems such as library circulation systems or large databases offer a wide range of functions. Some of these functions may not be implemented for policy or management reasons. Staff who operate the systems need clear guidelines on what they are and are not permitted to do with the system. Rules are needed for ensuring that data entry is consistent. Rules are needed for security reasons on who can access what and how on the system.

The project manager is responsible for making the team work together to achieve its objectives. Although the manager will require sufficient technical knowledge to be able to differentiate technical truth from fiction the management role is the more important. This combination of technical and managerial skills is often difficult to find. An active manager might prefer not to be taken out of the everyday politics of organizational management to work full time on a technical project. A technician may not be the best person to manage a project, despite having a genuine knowledge of IT systems.

A technical expert is needed on the project to develop a thorough understanding of the supplier's product, to search out and report any bugs in the system by an effective programme of testing, and to provide continuity when the system is operational. More than one will be needed for a large implementation. There will be a need for expertise in hardware and also software. This latter might range from familiarity with proprietary applications to programming knowledge, network administration and system design.

Another key member of a team is the end user – a member of

staff who will be using the system on a day-to-day basis when it is in operation. In fact, the more users there are on the team the better so that a broad range of operational needs can be identified and satisfied. Such users may be brought into the team at different stages as the project progresses.

Trade unions and IT agreements

It is essential that some agreement is reached with trade unions over the introduction of IT systems. Many organizations have formal IT agreements with trade unions that lay down guidelines for the use of IT. Although it has become accepted that IT can enhance working conditions, improve staff productivity and provide people with more marketable skills, there is still the possibility that industrial action could disrupt an expensive project at its most critical stage just as it is about to be implemented. The operational use of the system is the thing that most concerns trade union members. There are specific regulations concerning the use of VDU screens, the furniture used to house them and the physical conditions under which they are operated. These factors must be taken into account in designing a complex system so that there is no possibility of the implementation being delayed at the last moment, causing maximum disruption to services.

The specification process
Specifications

An operational specification is needed for any large project. The specification should outline in detail what the project will do for the library service. It is inevitable that once written a specification will be frozen in time. New developments in IT will have come along by the time it is finally implemented. However, the point of a specification is that it provides a clearly defined set of objectives to be achieved based upon the needs of the library service as expressed in its IT strategy. The specification will form the basis of the tender document for suppliers.

The specification should describe all the functions that the system is expected to perform. Essential core functions should be separated from those that are desirable or nice to have if possible. The specification should include details of such performance elements as response times, fallback conditions and system failure. Network conditions will need to be specified. The mixture of facilities required at different network terminals needs to be detailed. An easy way to get around the difficulty of writing a document for the first time is to borrow one from another library service that has itself recently gone through the same process. Some proprietary systems have active user groups which can advise on specifications. It saves time and effort in re-inventing the wheel if library services which have taken a lead in introducing a new system are consulted to find out what they did right and what they did wrong. Some suppliers will recommend that potential customers talk to their existing customers to gain a better understanding of the operational aspects of a system. A range of such customers will give an indication not only of the operational quality of a system but also of the competence of the supplier in installing and maintaining it.

Tendering

The network or system specification will form the basis of the tender to suppliers. Before a tender is advertised final approval must have been given by senior management to the specification. The relevant finance must have been secured for the full implementation and running of the system and the commitment obtained to provide the resources for the project team.

Tendering is now subject to EU law for public organizations including local authorities, government departments and bodies such as universities. Any contracts over a certain limit must go out to public tender. At the time of writing that limit was set at £180,000. This means that many IT projects would come under the legislation.

The tender document will include a number of elements besides the specification. The document needs to state whether maintenance will be performed by the supplier, in-house or by a third party. This might be split between software and hardware. Some libraries which are part of larger corporate bodies may have corporate policies to follow. If library staff will be responsible for operating the system then their training must be included in the document. Most IT systems are under continuous development and it might be the case that a supplier's system will have been updated between the time the specification was drawn up and the system is installed. The tender must allow some flexibility for such changes which would usually be improvements to the operational system.

Tender selection

Tenderers should be asked to submit a short proposal which will outline not only a description of their systems and their technical competence but a description of the company, its financial situation and viability, its customers including leading sites where the systems can be seen fully operational, and the numbers and range of staff available to work on the project.

Shortlisting may not be difficult in circumstances where there are few suppliers of specialized systems. The market leader will always be a preferred option. The leader will usually have a reputation for having a better product, a more advanced system which is likely to last longer or a larger operation with more staff who are able to deal with problems more quickly. A supplier who has performed well in the past will be preferred over an unknown. There may be reasons for shortlisting newer companies who are genuinely innovative, enthusiastic or hungry for business and which may give better service than larger companies which have dozens or even hundreds of contracts to deal with.

The shortlisted contenders should be examined in more detail. Talking to existing customers is valuable, although it is misleading to rely purely on anecdotal evidence. A performance test of a system is essential to test the claims of the supplier. This should take place under conditions similar to those expected in practice. For a library circulation control system this might mean a test on a database of a comparable size and configuration. This might take place on the supplier's premises or on those of an existing customer. It is in any case useful to inspect a supplier's premises to see if the claims in the tender seem accurate. Testing out a network is obviously difficult because no two networks are alike so some impression needs to be gained of the different hardware and software available. Different forms of intelligence to be consulted include: manufacturers' literature; the industry press, especially test reports in journals; user groups if they exist; bulletin boards and newsgroups on the Internet; the general grapevine. The more that is known about the industry and the more contacts developed the easier it is to make an informed choice.

Suppliers tend to offer standard IT solutions and any localized variations may be more costly to implement. The ideal specification might have to be modified to avoid excessive extra costs. Fewer and fewer systems these days are tailored to specific customers, most are ready made and customers have to adapt their requirements accordingly. This need not be a problem with mature systems where suppliers have built in most of the requirements of customers based upon years of experience.

Meeting the supplier's staff that will be responsible for the installation and operation of a system is useful. Presentations and demonstrations by suppliers to a range of staff in the library service, including those who will be using the system, can be useful for nit-picking any problems which might have implications for operational management. Ease of use, response times of databases, the amount of training required, the level of online support, documentation etc. can be assessed.

A supplier will be chosen on a number of criteria, not just on the cost, although there is always a tendency to effect the cheapest possible deal. The tenders should be subjected to a rigorous analysis with points given for an agreed set of criteria. Tenders which offer more than the required specification may be given more points but the important point is to ensure that all the requirements of the specification are met. Accepting lower performance in order to save money or to obtain extra frills may turn out to be a bad decision if the system fails to operate effectively.

The contract

Suppliers often have standard contracts for their systems. These should be examined in great detail and legal advice sought to clarify any restrictions and conditions. Once signed it is a legally binding commitment on both parties so the contents must be clearly understood and agreed with confidence.

Warranty

The contract should include information about maintenance and warranty. The warranty should be a reassurance that the system will function according to the agreed specification and any equipment or software problems that prevent this will be put right at the supplier's expense. A warranty normally runs for a specific period, often 12 months, and is generally tied in to a final payment on the system which is a proportion of the contract value, often up to 15%. A warranty is not the same as a maintenance contract, which should come into operation as the warranty period expires. Original contracts may include a maintenance element valid for a specific period after the system has become operational. Renewal of this maintenance contract will almost certainly be essential to the future operation of the system unless the maintenance is to be carried out in-house. Provision should have been made for the revenue costs of this maintenance before the system was put out to tender.

Updates

Updates to a system will become necessary and some provision will be needed for them. They may be standard improvements or additional desirable features. They may be generated as requests from the customer or proffered by the supplier based upon changes in software or hardware performance. Few systems remain static. The more flexible the system the more likely it is to change over time. The growth in networks has been spectacular in recent years and many networks designed for limited functions have had many other additions forced on to them. Library circulation control systems now often share their networks with CD-ROMs, in-house databases and many other applications. Updates to major systems with large databases can be inconvenient, with long periods of downtime when data is being transferred or sorted or is otherwise unavailable. Errors can creep into the process and data can become corrupted. New updates are best avoided until they have been tested and proved workable elsewhere.

Specification into practice

The specification must be translated into a working document to be agreed by the supplier and the customer. It should contain the details of all the functions the system will carry out. For an off-the-shelf system it is likely that the documentation already exists, in which case it must be checked carefully to make sure that the system fulfils the functions required of it. The document will list all the functions and how the system performs them. It should include an overview of the system design, design standards and details of the interconnections of different parts of the system. This may include: terminals, networks and other hardware elements, preferably in a schematized diagram; database details, inputs, outputs and forms; transaction details, responses, manual or automatic transactions, transactions that are allowed and those that are not allowed; system parameters, performance details etc. Details of the support facilities should be included.

Changes to the specification

No matter how detailed the initial specification has been and how much time has been spent on it, there will inevitably be a desire to introduce changes as experience shows up unanticipated operational problems or difficulties. Some of these difficulties will relate to the way the system operates, which is obviously different from any manual systems in use before. Working practices imposed by the system, whether it is a simple desktop computer running standard office software or a complex network in a large library service, will require a change in behaviour by the users of the system.

Sometimes this may have the effect of increasing the workload in other areas. One example of this is stock control. In many libraries the old card catalogue was often inaccurate, out of date and did not represent the true picture of books on the shelves. A computerized database requires much more stringent control. Stock on shelves must match the database more accurately and regular stock control must be undertaken if the database is not to become out of date. One of the main reasons for this is that users are able to see more clearly what items are in stock and to place orders for them. A great deal of time can be wasted searching for non-existent items if the database is inaccurate. The extra burden of stock control may come as a shock to some libraries that have never given this priority before.

With a desktop system the discipline of file and directory control has to be imposed and users need to get used to entering all their ideas straight on to the screen in order to take advantage of the efficiencies of using electronic text. The discipline imposed by electronic systems comes as a surprise to many users and some find this kind of working difficult to adjust to.

Any changes required must be negotiated with the supplier. There is a danger that changes may provide an excuse for a supplier to move more slowly on implementation. Minor changes are best bundled together into a single request later so that the project is not being constantly held up. Regular meetings with the supplier's project team should be used to monitor progress on the implementation and deal with any problems arising.

Installation
Physical work

Hardware is usually installed first but in many cases with off-the-shelf systems software comes pre-loaded on to the computers. An installation plan is needed to ensure that everything runs smoothly and the project timetable is adhered to. There are many elements included in this process. Electrical power supplies must be planned and installed if the system is more than a simple desktop computer. The work may involve the need for redecoration or other work in public areas which must be done before the project can progress any further. A large network may require extensive cabling which will involve site surveys and route maps.

Equipment must be delivered safely, stored securely and handled carefully. Space will need to be found for large items. Building surveys may be needed for large items and routes worked out for moving equipment without mishap or damage. A system may need to be put in place piece by piece and cannot be effectively tested until all the parts are connected. Floor loading may need to be taken into account and the environmental conditions in which the equipment is to operate, although most modern systems are designed to work in a normal office environment..

The working conditions of staff who will be responsible for day-to-day operation and maintenance of the system must not be overlooked in the siting of equipment and its accessibility. Lighting, heating and other factors must be taken into account, as well as health and safety considerations.

The supplier and his contractors or sub-contractors must be given rights of access to do their work and this may involve security clearance.

Configuring and testing

The testing of any system, however small, is necessary and time must be allocated for it in any project. The purpose of testing is to find any problems and there must be time to deal with these before successive stages of the project can be completed. Staff and resources are needed for testing and this must be accounted for in the overall IT strategy.

Testing may take place even before equipment is installed, on the supplier's premises. It will be commenced in earnest when most of the system has been physically installed. The initial testing will be done to make sure the equipment and software are working properly. Systems built around a database may have a test database installed and a programme of tests will need to be run against the new system to see if it is working to expectations. This confidence testing is also useful for developing a more detailed knowledge and a realistic picture of what the system can and cannot do, as opposed to the vague, idealized image promoted by the supplier's sales and marketing staff. The testing may be divided into different types. There will be tests to assess the performance of the system followed by tests to examine a matrix of functions to ensure that they are all working, or at least all the important functions are working. Detailed scripts are often used to test combinations of functions. With sophisticated systems there may be too many functions to be tested in combination to cover them all. In this case there should be tests to see how the system copes with extreme situations.

Systems require configuration as part of the installation. Some systems have an excess of sophisticated functions, not all of which will be needed. These systems must be configured to provide those functions that are wanted and to close off those that are not. A library may want the facility of issuing items from a short-loan collection, for example, while another does not. A public library may wish to distinguish between adult and children's fiction for lending purposes, whereas an academic library may wish to distinguish between staff and student loans. All of these settings must be configured to work automatically so the operational staff do not have to consult extensive lists of rules every time they issue an item. Needless to say, configuration has to be tested to make sure it is working correctly without errors and confusion.

Testing networks is also important to ensure that there have been no mistakes in installation, that the performance of the network is up to expectations, that all the different cables, routers and other devices are working properly. Individual terminals need to be tested as they are brought into use to access facilities such as CD-ROMs.

The final testing is acceptance testing in which the customer will effectively sign off the system as conforming to the specification and working to the agreed standard. This is also a point at which staged payments may be made and the customer must feel confident that the system meets the library service's requirements. The acceptance testing should be carried out in conditions which are effectively those that would exist during operational use of the system. Staff who have been trained on the system should carry out the testing, reporting any discrepancies they find for final correction by the supplier.

Desktop computers bought off the shelf with standard software are usually set up for working fairly quickly and present few problems. The main problems come from users who are not familiar with the software or hardware and need support after their initial training. Hardware problems are usually spotted fairly quickly. Software packages are generally reliable and the tendency is to deliver them on CD-ROM for easy installation, especially on networks.

Larger systems will almost always have bugs which must be brought to the attention of the supplier. Large databases provide many opportunities for problems to creep in during installation, especially if the system software is relatively new or has been changed since the last installation was made for a previous customer. No two customer configurations are the same even though they may be using the same software. Complex networks will have more opportunities for bugs to develop. Most network operating software is now designed for remote detection of problems and errors so that network operators can trace them more easily without having to walk round the whole of the network.

A library service introducing a large IT system, even a so-called turnkey system, will have many tasks to complete in conjunction with the supplier. Both will be working to a strict implementation timetable with a long chain of events. In such a situation many things can occur which might delay the implementation. The customer has a responsibility to meet deadlines just as much as the supplier and it is important that this responsibility is carried out effectively so that the supplier is not given an excuse for poor performance on the project. In many ways the customer is under more pressure than the supplier to deliver its side of the bargain. It is essential therefore that adequate resources are provided for implementation on the customer side and that the timetable is followed.

Progress meetings

Regular meetings between customer and supplier staff are needed to ensure that the implementation is proceeding to plan. A detailed agenda is needed so that actions can be agreed unambiguously, minuted and subsequent performance in carrying out those actions monitored. Any later conflicts about responsibility for delays or unsolved bugs and problems can then be tested against the documented action points. In the implementation of complex systems, even when these are supposed to be turnkey systems there are bound to be unforeseen hitches, grey areas and baffling problems. The customer needs to be careful that there are no loopholes through which the supplier might avoid blame or worse still apportion the blame to the customer.

Training
Types of training

An IT strategy must include plans for training people in any new systems being introduced. There may be a need for several different groups of people to be trained. IT support staff will require training in operating systems, network maintenance, software management, database management and other topics depending on the range of IT facilities. The operational staff who use the library's IT systems will require training in day-to-day routines and simple troubleshooting. There may be people who need training in the input of information to a large database such as a financial management system and others who need training in retrieval. Distributed information held on servers such as Web pages and stored documents will need to be input and maintained by staff with more specialized skills. With a small desktop system there may be only one person who needs to be trained in all of these functions. The larger the system the more likely it is that these tasks will be separated out and delegated to separate groups or individuals.

Library service training

The supplier should be responsible for the initial training and may organize this for the different tasks as indicated above. This round of training will apply to staff who will later act as instructors to their colleagues in the library service. It is important that they are chosen as much for their training skills as their IT expertise as technical experts do not always make the best trainers. Timing is important; there should not be a long delay between training and the operational use of the system but neither should training be left to the last minute when people may be under pressure to deal with unforeseen operational problems. Staff should also be allowed time away from the pressures and distractions of their everyday work to concentrate on their training. A separate training room or training facility is a distinct advantage.

The IT strategy must emphasize the importance of training and should include planned programmes for training staff and users.

Risks

Implementation is not without risks and these must be understood if the implementation programme is to be kept on track. Risks encountered may include:

☐ unexpected, unforeseen consequences
☐ delays and breakdowns
☐ loss of commitment before completion
☐ conflicting priorities not identified in time
☐ resources and finance not available when required
☐ loss or transfer of key project team members
☐ failure to gain complete approval for individual projects
☐ organizational resistance to the speed or extent of change.

The main consequences of any of these risks are likely to be delays in implementation. In practice, implementation nearly always takes longer than expected. An IT strategy must allow for delays and frustrations. There must be some flexibility built into the timetable to cope with potential delays. Extra resources should be held in reserve to be brought in if needed and management action taken as swiftly as possible to deal with the problem. Temporary service closures must be prepared for in extreme cases.

Barriers to implementing a strategy

There are a number of factors which may prevent the complete and successful implementation of the strategy which could include:

☐ difficulties in measuring the benefits and therefore justifying the investment costs
☐ the nature of the library service, its traditions and culture
☐ difficulties in recruiting the right staff
☐ interdepartmental politics
☐ trade union objections
☐ lack of finance
☐ the 'millstone' legacy of existing IT systems
☐ insufficient resources for staff training
☐ inadequate infrastructure to cope with major system changes
☐ negative attitudes of staff which undermine the benefits
☐ technology that may be of only limited use in dealing with some organizational problems

These factors must be assessed beforehand and steps taken where possible to mitigate the negative effects.

References

1 Price, Stan, *Managing computer projects*, London, Wiley, 1986.
2 Currie, Wendy, 'Outsourcing in the private and public sectors: an unpredictable IT strategy', *European journal of information systems*, **4**, 1996, 226–36.

10 Monitoring and review

It is a bad plan that admits of no modification.

Publius Syrus[1]

Objectives

☐ **Plan monitoring activities**
☐ **Measure benefits of new IT facilities**
☐ **Continue to monitor external developments**
☐ **Plan the review process**
☐ **Deal with failures.**

Monitoring
Internal and external

There are two main aspects to monitoring : internal and external. Internal monitoring is essential to assess the effectiveness of the strategy as it is implemented. It is designed to measure effectiveness by looking at system use and user reactions. It is important to monitor the changes which continue to take place in the external environment which can affect the implementation as it is carried out and may lead to changes being undertaken during the process. A simple example of this might be the appearance of a much-improved version of software which would make a system more flexible and easier to use. On the other hand, some processes that provide links to the external world may become obsolete as fashions change. One example is the continuing shift from Telnet and Gopher to World Wide Web access for information retrieval on the Internet, including access to library catalogues.

Uncertainties

The introduction of new IT systems can be an uncertain process. A system can affect an organization in a number of different ways some of which will not be properly understood until afterwards. The uncertainty is the result of several things. The costs, benefits and risks are difficult to forecast accurately and are often intangible and difficult to disentangle from the more general effects of other innovations or externally induced changes upon the organization. Many new systems represent new ways of doing things and comparisons with previous methods cannot be made. New systems are genuine innovations for the organization and may have a profound effect upon the culture and the social structures of the organization beyond their immediate application.

The timescale in planning a new system is always likely to be longer than the timescale upon which reasonably accurate forecasts about the environment can be made. This means that events are almost certain to overtake any new system before it is fully implemented. Measuring the effects of the introduction of the system will thus take place in different circumstances to those in which it was planned.

Some systems can actually alter the organization's boundary with its external environment by changing its relationships with users, suppliers, its competitors and its principal funding authority. Libraries are beginning to link up together for mutual benefit and this may result in stronger links than those between the library and its parent organization. New users who never set foot inside it before may be attracted to a library when new IT facilities are introduced. These users may be interested only in the IT systems though some may be persuaded to use the more traditional facilities of the library.

After the initial impact of the introduction of the new system there may be secondary effects produced which give rise to unpredictable results. If new systems are introduced as part of a more general change programme it may be difficult to ascertain which changes led to a particular outcome. New systems often serve different groups of users and it is often difficult to allocate costs and benefits between them.

As a result of all this the benefits may not be realized in the way expected. Benefits may not be spread as evenly as expected because use of the system is not uniform, with some staff making greater use than others because they are better informed or trained. Benefits can be lost through poor management. They can also be lost because the conditions that originally made them seem attractive have changed.

Internal monitoring
Assessing benefits

In the section in Chapter 9 on evaluation a number of questions were suggested for the evaluation of the potential success of the IT strategy prior to being implemented. After implementation these questions will need to be re-examined to see if the strategy is living up to its expectations. The benefits that were predicted will need to be confirmed in the monitoring process.

Mintzberg's organizational model

In order to avoid some of the problems of measuring the benefits resulting from the introduction of new IT facilities it is helpful to use a framework of benefits that can be applied across the organization. To do this Farbey suggests that it is worth looking at Mintzberg's model for the organization which is divided into five distinct parts.[2,3]

At the top of the organization is the strategic apex. This is the senior management stratum where the main policies are formulated and the direction of the organization is decided.

At the tactical or middle management stratum Mintzberg proposed three separate areas. Firstly, the classic middle management layer, concerned with directing and controlling the organization's agreed objectives. Secondly, the support staff which provides assistance to others, particularly managers, to enable them to do their work efficiently. Thirdly, there is the so-called technostructure or technical infrastructure, which provides the means by which information can flow freely through the organization to aid both operational activities and management decision making.

Finally, at the base of Mintzberg's theoretical pyramid is the operational stratum, where services are provided directly to users. At this level activities are easier to measure in terms of quantities, such as issues of books on a circulation system.

Using Mintzberg's divisions as a framework to examine benefits it is possible to look at the effects IT systems have had on each of the five parts.

Strategic benefits of IT systems

Starting at the strategic management level, we would look for benefits which include those directly concerned with the organization's overall strategy:

☐ How far have the organization's operational boundaries been extended?
☐ How far have internal functions been integrated?
☐ Have any significant cooperative projects been developed?
☐ Has the organization been given a lead or a competitive edge?
☐ Have new services been developed?
☐ Has the infrastructure of the organization been successfully developed?

One overriding reason for introducing new IT systems may be to defend the long-term viability of the library service. IT has equipped competitors to offer services that were traditionally the preserve of libraries and educational bodies. Individuals using home computers linked to telephone lines can now link into vast databases of information on the Internet. For some this may satisfy all their needs. As the range of information grows and its accessibility improves more people will be content to find information in this way. The attraction is that this is a convenient, relatively cheap and speedy means of access to information. In the same way it is possible to download educational materials and tutorials on many subjects. Before long it will be possible to undertake major courses of study without entering a university or college. Libraries and academic institutions must be aware of competition for their services and must be one step ahead in order to deal with the problem.

IT may be able to permit the library service to regenerate itself to provide new services which will attract users. The Internet is an opportunity as well as a threat. Libraries can become information providers in their own right, making unique sources of information available or helping to organize the Internet to make it easier to use. By keeping up with new IT developments, library services can demonstrate that they have the knowledge and ability to keep their users at the leading edge of developments. New IT services have been shown to attract new users who would not previously have used a library and who now use it only to access the IT services. Measurement of user activity and take up of new services will be obvious measures used to assess benefits.

Sometimes the motivation for new systems is necessity, the feeling that without them the library service may not have a longer term future. This is becoming true for more and more organizations as new information structures with improved delivery of information such as the World Wide Web overtake traditional ones such as libraries and learning centres.

Public sector organizations have been subject to competition through enforced changes and the idea of compulsory competitive tendering has been suggested for public libraries and IT support services in the UK. The introduction into libraries of advanced IT systems that provide economies of scale and an infrastructure for future growth could provide a competitive edge for the staff of a library service bidding for the contract to run these services.

Management benefits

At the next level of the organization there is a need to assess the benefits to management efficiency and effectiveness. The following questions should be asked:

☐ Has the availability of management information and performance data improved?
☐ Is decision making better?
☐ Are resources allocated more effectively?
☐ Is there better internal standardization?
☐ Is there better internal control and understanding of operations?
☐ Has flexibility increased?
☐ Have there been improvements in staff management and development?

An example of improved flexibility is a piece of electronic text being used for a number of different purposes: first as an e-mail message, then incorporated into a word-processed report and later manipulated using a DTP system to produce a publicity flyer. IT systems often enable staff to be more creative. The time saved in the basic production of documents with IT may with more sophisticated software be used to produce a better looking, more professional result. People find new ways of working using IT and new posts may be created to capitalize on these benefits. A recent example is the rash of Webmasters who are being appointed to establish and maintain library pages on the World Wide Web.

Improved management and development of staff should result from the increased motivation which learning and the application of new skills can bring. IT systems can make work more interesting and varied by providing better communication, improved access to information and more ways to manipulate information to produce a more personalized output. The marketable skills of employees can be increased by their training in and use of IT.

A better understanding of the way in which the organization operates internally should be matched by a better idea of the external environment and the organization's place within it. Access to more information about the external environment, through e-mail contacts with colleagues in peer organizations or through better information obtained through online systems, should help this.

Improved communications within the library service should be expected, with consequent improvements in understanding of roles by staff, more democratic decision making based on more open information, increased knowledge and an improved mental image of the library service.

In order to assess the effects of the strategy surveys of users will be needed to determine whether the strategy has produced the benefits expected. This may include both internal staff users and external client users. The aim will be to find out if people have taken up the opportunities offered by the strategy and whether this has had a positive effect on their work, communication and attitudes.

Support benefits

Improvements in support services might include:

☐ better financial control
☐ better information with more up to date reports for budget tracking
☐ better cost-centred management
☐ improved knowledge of costs and benefits of different operations

☐ improved access to human resources information.

In many organizations IT systems have acted as the driving force for changes in the support structure itself, with posts being restructured around the new procedures for input, maintenance and output from computerized financial or personnel systems. Once one level of IT has been introduced and staff have become used to the idea of using IT and feel confident about learning more, it is often easier to introduce further systems.

Benefits from an improved technical infrastructure

An improved infrastructure can bring many benefits. The benefits of electronic networking, using e-mail for example, should include:

☐ improvements in general communication
☐ better group and project working
☐ the involvement of more people in decision making
☐ the creation of a better consensus for resulting actions
☐ the quicker production and circulation of reports
☐ the need for fewer meetings and less travel.

Improvements in the quality of finished documents and their presentation can enhance their legibility and acceptability and provide the basis for better decision making and negotiating.

Once the infrastructure has been established it should be capable of extension and addition without too much extra expenditure. Extra servers can be added to a network, including CD-ROM and Intranet servers as well as databases for improved information retrieval.

The formalized information infrastructure represented above is not the whole picture of information flow in the organization. One of the main influences on an organization is information that comes from the informal structure and includes the unwritten rules and procedures for dealing with outsiders such as users, suppliers and funding bodies. Relationships with these may occasionally be formalized, for example in customer charters, specification documents or agreed service plans, but much of the day-to-day dealings follow unwritten though tacitly accepted rules to which all parties adhere. Communication is through human interaction and the development of relationships which are negotiated between the parties. Unquantifiable but important social and political factors can influence these relationships. Better and faster communication can help to create an improved image of the library service among staff and with external users.

Operational benefits

New systems are generally introduced with the aim of improving the efficiency and effectiveness of operational services. A saving in time on basic transactions in a library such as shaving a few seconds off the discharge of a book returned by a user can add up to a large amount of time saved in a year. Improved performance and productivity of staff should be expected. At the same time IT can be expected to increase the range of possibilities offered for routine services, improving the quality of operations at a reduced cost. The difference between a computerized catalogue, with its ability to search for information through authors, titles, keywords and other fields, and a card catalogue arranged simply by author is just one example of the power of IT to enrich basic operations.

Increased services for users may be offered such as self-renewal of books, the ability to reserve books themselves through a terminal and even to order interlibrary loans. Staff can summon up information on their enquiry screens more quickly in response to requests from users and give accurate information about the status of books on loan and their expected return dates.

For some tasks easier operation may lead to de-skilling and a subsequent saving if less experienced staff can be employed. Improvements in the efficiency of acquisition of materials and other inputs may be expected with a faster turnaround of items. Greater exploitation through increased use of those materials may be expected and thus the outputs in terms of issues of books etc. would also be expected show an improvement.

Costs may be reduced over a range of headings including those for storage and accommodation. The change from using printed copies to CD-ROMs can have a dramatic effect upon storage space and other costs. In Manchester Central Library the move from paper copies of British and European patents to CD-ROM versions has enabled thousands of feet of shelf space to be freed up. Several years of patents can now be stored in a small cabinet on open access compared with bulky printed versions which had to be stored in remote stacks and physically retrieved upon demand.

IT may also generate extra income for the service. Many libraries are now introducing charged services for Internet, charges for printouts from CD-ROMs, sales of shareware and blank floppy disks. Value-added services such as information research from CD-ROMs and online services, including the packaging of results in an easy to use portfolio, can generate further income and enhance the image of the service to users, especially businesses.

A better image of the library service in the eyes of all users should be generated with improvements in services.

External monitoring
New technological developments

Previous chapters have indicated the need for research in the IT marketplace. IT is constantly changing. There is a need for constant monitoring of new developments and improvements to see if any further opportunities arise. Once the main foundation has been laid it can be built up in stages. As expertise develops within an organization new developments become easier to add on. The learning curves are less dramatic for new software and productivity benefits can occur more quickly. It is rare that completely new programs arrive unexpectedly. A lot of new software is designed to improve the functionality of existing programs. Standardization on Windows has allowed many more new programs to succeed because users have already gained experience in the basic principles of their operation through using other Windows programs.

Suppliers and their competitors should be monitored for new developments. If a rival system has been updated and improved then the library's own supplier can be expected to match the improvement.

The trend in hardware has been towards continually increasing power per unit cost. This means that functions which were impossible to achieve on desktop machines in the past are becoming routine. Monitoring should look for inexpensive ways to give users more power, speed and flexibility which will help to improve productivity further.

Political and economic challenges

Although this is always a particular concern of senior management, the implications for IT should also be monitored. The present political interest in the development of the information society and its social and economic consequences has produced a wide range of initiatives aimed at businesses, education, information providers and others. Opportunities have been created for innovative services, for the transition from older systems to new ones. Much effort and money is being devoted to the mitigation of the effects of obsolescence on industry and society. More opportunities will open up in the future for those libraries and information services that can seek them out.

National and international developments

The social changes generated by the move towards an information society will mean an increased need for training and education, for information gathering and interpretation, for more efficient communication and a wider range of choices in every service activity. Swift adoption of new technology, especially software, creates waves of change at a national and international level.

Globalization is already occurring in many industries and activities. Using the Internet to keep up to date with new developments is part of the globalization process. It is said that 90% of all scientists who have ever lived are now on the Internet. Many new developments are reported first on the Internet, ideas circulate quickly, experiences are shared and research projects altered in the light of this new information. In this way developments are speeded up and original ideas can be adopted around the world in weeks or even days.

Being aware of trends, riding along with them, keeping ahead will become qualities by which a library service is judged.

Review
The review process

The review process is essentially one involving feedback. The results of monitoring the strategy are analysed and conclusions drawn about the effectiveness of the strategy. This information is used to shift the strategy towards a more effective direction. Nonproductive activities or facilities should be phased out or re-examined to determine why they have failed to gain support. Effort and resources should be redirected and concentrated on areas where demand is greatest. Complaints and failures should be examined carefully and problems dealt with.

Intervals

The IT strategy should be re-examined at regular intervals. Some funding bodies demand an annual statement which is designed to fit in with the annual budget and service planning. An annual cycle may be too long for some IT projects considering the rapid changes which take place in IT. Equipment has a shorter and shorter life. Some items of hardware may become out of date almost before they are delivered and installed. Software can become obsolete in a few months. Timing is essential when large orders are being placed. An impending upgrade to an operating system may delay a large purchase so that the full benefits can be assessed before an investment is made.

Updating the strategy

Updating a strategy is obviously easier than developing the original strategy but it is not just a case of tinkering with a few of the project plans. The strategy will need to be refined as knowledge and expertise increases. There may be a need to re-examine the original aims and objectives. The priority of some projects may need to be changed in the light of experience and as a response to external developments. Some medium- or longer-term aims may be overtaken by events and lose their relevance altogether.

Failure management

Although careful planning should have ensured successful outcomes, some projects may have failed. It is unlikely that a project will fail completely but it may fall short of some of the expected outcomes. Any failures need to be examined carefully to discover the causes so that corrections can be made to try to recover the projects. The lessons learned can be put into practice in future projects.

Reasons for failure may include:

- ☐ unreasonably high expectations
- ☐ uncontrollable circumstances
- ☐ inadequate management of the strategy
- ☐ inadequate implementation
- ☐ user resistance
- ☐ inadequate specification.

One of the main failures in implementing projects is often an under-estimate of the time needed for full implementation and acceptance. There is a tendency to be optimistic or to react to pressures for a speedy implementation which fails because the organization is not ready to assimilate a new or a radical way of working.

References

1 Publius Syrus, *Maxim 469*.
2 Farbey, Barbara, Land, Frank and Targett, David, *How to assess your IT investment: a study of methods and practice*, Oxford, Butterworth, 1993.
3 Mintzberg, Henry, *The structuring of organizations*, Englewood Cliffs, Prentice Hall, 1979.

11 Future strategy for libraries

The danger of the past was that men became slaves. The danger of the future is that men may become robots.

Erich Fromm[1]

Objectives

- ☐ **Develop flexible IT strategies that can adapt to change**
- ☐ **Develop an awareness of future IT developments that might affect library IT strategies**
- ☐ **Consider social changes and their possible impact on library and information services.**

The future

Increasing change

The future is created by what people do. It is the sum of all the actions people take. To this extent individuals and organizations can ensure themselves a part in the future. The world has become so complex, however, that no one can predict the eventual outcome of their actions. Many other actions will impinge upon them. Within an organization it may be possible to exert some degree of control over the way it functions through internal action. Externally the process is more difficult because events are beyond its control.

Libraries, as intermediaries, are dependent upon the actions of suppliers of information on the one hand and users of information on the other.

In trying to predict future trends libraries can monitor in detail most of their internal transactions and activities. A profile can be built up of the use of a library network, for example:

- ☐ the rate of use of terminals
- ☐ the volume of individual database or CD-ROM access
- ☐ volumes of network traffic
- ☐ daily use patterns
- ☐ individual user access.

Predictions of future use can then be made. Once the network is made available for external access monitoring may become less useful and patterns less predictable. The increasing trend towards inter-networking may exacerbate the situation.

Internal measures provide limited local information about trends. Libraries must also look beyond their own internal environments towards trends in the IT marketplace, political and social trends, legislation and changes in the information gathering and using habits of their users.

Change has become a self-generating process in which waves of change create further changes on an ever-widening front. The more people who link into the Internet, the more ideas will be generated, and the more facilities will be created. This will in turn attract more people to it. More people are working with electronic information and more jobs are being created in information work. The information content of all jobs is increasing. The information society is one in which most people will earn their living through information and be involved in accessing, using and creating information. This means that libraries must adapt to change rather than ignore it in the hope that it will not affect them.

- ☐ Libraries must attempt to predict the future to some extent if they are to plan beyond the short term.
- ☐ Libraries and information services have a role to play in the information society and must look for opportunities to develop that role.
- ☐ Libraries should not only follow change, they should be actively involved in developing change themselves as a means of keeping ahead of potential rivals.
- ☐ Libraries must build into their future strategies the concept of continual change.

Increasing complexity

The growth in information and communication looks set to continue for the foreseeable future. The problem of the 'information explosion' – much discussed in the 1980s but seemingly superseded by other concerns – is still with us. The number of books published continues to rise each year, as does the number of periodicals. The World Wide Web has provided another huge outlet for electronic publishing, allowing individuals for the first time the opportunity to present their ideas to the world.

The increasing, often bewildering choices presented by niche products from a multiplicity of outlets indicates how complex modern life is becoming. Information is generated at every stage of the research, design, manufacture, marketing and sale of products. But information is not just a by-product of other activities; it has become an important product in its own right. Far from helping to deal with the problem of complexity, information is actually contributing towards it.

What seems certain about the future is that there will be greater complexity and an increasing fragmentation of knowledge into narrower specialist areas, generating more information and the need for more connections.

☐ Libraries will need to connect into more networks.
☐ Libraries will need to provide more ways for their users to access information.
☐ Libraries will need to offer a wider range of services.
☐ Libraries will have to be prepared to take on take on more functions.

Increasing uncertainty

As the number of possible choices increases so decisions become more difficult and research becomes more expensive and time-consuming. The development of interconnected networks is likely to increase uncertainty because the behaviour of complex networks is more difficult to predict. Although modern systems are generally reliable, tracing faults when things go wrong on a complex network can be very difficult.

As information increases on open networks such as the World Wide Web its authenticity and authority becomes less easy to establish. Few controls exist over the accuracy of information published in this way. The ease and speed with which information can be copied and transmitted elsewhere means that inaccuracies are perpetuated and often become accepted as fact. The quality of information cannot be guaranteed.

All of these developments pose problems for libraries as information providers. The struggle to keep pace with new developments in information will be more difficult in the future but librarians are well placed as users and gatekeepers to exploit information better than others.

☐ Libraries have a role to play as well-established organizers of information in counteracting confusion and uncertainty.
☐ Libraries have a role as advisers and helpers in the information gathering process which will be in more demand than ever.

Hardware developments
Increasing variety

The range of IT products is increasing and the continued development and refinement of existing devices seems inexorable. The continued shortening of product life cycles means that upgraded and improved equipment is continually flowing on to the market. Some large organizations have taken to skipping upgrades and jumping generations of products rather than replace all their equipment every couple of years.

Among the new devices now appearing are:

☐ Network computers – stripped down computers designed as terminals connected to powerful servers.
☐ DVD-ROM – digital video disks offering 4.7 Gb storage, enough to hold two hours of full motion full-screen video and destined to replace CD-ROMs and video recorders.
☐ MO – magneto-optical disks with 6 to 7 Gb storage.
☐ Digital cameras – for instant electronic image capture. Images can be downloaded straight into a computer and used in multimedia documents, Web pages etc.
☐ Wireless – keyboards, mice, laptop computers and other devices can transmit data to a PC without cables using infra-red.

☐ Palmtops and PDAs – small handheld pocket computers and personal digital assistants, useful for making notes in the field and at meetings or when travelling, which can be downloaded to a desktop PC for further processing.

All of these products have potential applications in libraries and some are already being introduced.

☐ Libraries should maintain awareness of the potential of new IT products.
☐ Libraries should continue to introduce innovative technology to improve services and facilities.

Increasing speed

Faster, more powerful servers are being introduced that can provide application software as and when needed to network computers used as terminals. New multimedia microchips have now appeared that will improve the speed and quality of video applications. Parallel processing is likely to increase the speed of desktop computers and servers even further. The move towards ISDN and ATM for network communications is part of the inexorable desire for increased speed and a shortening of response times for information retrieval. A multiplying effect in performance is achieved as processors, CD-ROMs, video RAM, hard disks and other components are all given more power and speed. The move from 16-bit to 32-bit systems is taking place with the introduction of Windows 95, Windows NT and other software. The move to 64-bit systems will follow now that the newer domestic game systems are already using them.

Users will always be aware of faster systems in the marketplace. Home computers are now often faster than those in the workplace, a complete reversal of the situation a few years ago. There is always a danger that a library will appear to be second-rate and slow compared with information retrieval systems in the home or in other organizations. People soon become used to increases in the speed of computers and never cease to demand more. They will migrate towards the services that provide the quickest access to information.

- ☐ Libraries should incorporate the need for increased speed into their strategies by streamlining their activities and minimizing access procedures.
- ☐ Libraries should provide users with systems that deliver information as quickly as possible with the minimum of effort.

Increasing portability

The capacity of hard disks on desktop and laptop computers continues to increase. Removable hard disks are becoming more popular, although these are not yet small enough to be carried around from machine to machine with ease. At the same time new standards for floppy disks are increasing the storage capacity of pocketable media. In the future library users may carry around their own personal applications and files which they may want to use at terminals in the library. Alternatively they may use laptop computers which they will want to connect into the library network, either directly or remotely.

- ☐ Libraries may need to make provision for users to plug portable devices into library networks.

Increasing integration

The merging of functions and the blurring of boundaries between devices will continue in the future. Computers are already used for faxing, as answerphones, television and radio receivers and audio CD players. Computers can now process digital images captured from still cameras and camcorders and look set to replace conventional photographic products for many applications. Many domestic products are being computerized and new hybrid systems are being created. Internet television now appearing in the USA, for instance, uses a special decoder for a television, which allows access to an interactive channel for World Wide Web searching.

- ☐ Libraries may need to provide multifunctional terminals for users.
- ☐ Libraries will need to provide a wide range of communication facilities for users.

Software developments
Increasing sophistication

Software has become increasingly more powerful and the introduction of new applications has increased. Producing customized
programs has become easier with software development packages.
Distribution of new programs has become faster and easier with
the advent of the Internet and the growth of shareware. Software
is becoming available that can learn about the preferences of the
user and adapt itself accordingly. Intelligent agents are being
developed that will provide more precise information retrieval
from the Internet.

Retailing and banking systems have been designed to collect
and analyse transaction data in very sophisticated ways in order
to build up profiles of users and their needs. In supermarkets and
stores the systems are used for accurate measurement of stock
flow and stock control. This emphasis on deriving the maximum
amount of information from transaction processes is being carried
a stage further by the use of more intelligent database software
which can recognize trends and patterns buried deep in the data.
Such data-mining techniques could have useful applications in
libraries.

Shared software such as groupware is already changing the way
in which people work in small teams, coming together to solve
problems and develop projects. Voice messaging, video conferencing software and file transfer will enable this process to be carried
out in a much improved way in future. Libraries with scattered
sites will benefit from the ability to communicate more freely in
this way without the need to arrange costly and time-consuming
meetings at a single location. If users could make use of applications on the library network they might be provided with more
powerful resources and a wider range of facilities than they would
have on their own computers. Groups or communities could be provided with facilities to communicate and collaborate.

☐ Libraries could utilize intelligent software in the future to store
   profiles of user preferences so that users can be alerted to new
   items of interest.
☐ Libraries could make use of data-mining techniques to improve
   management information from transactional data.
☐ Libraries will need to provide more sophisticated facilities such

as video conferencing not only for their own staff but also for users.

☐ Libraries should provide access to computing facilities on their networks for library users, rather than just information access.

☐ Libraries could develop their networks as community resources rather than closed systems thereby helping to integrate the library more closely with the community it serves.

Increasing integration

The traditional interface to the library catalogue is changing. OPACs have been around for several years but have usually been menu-driven systems, which can be relatively slow and cumbersome to use. The introduction of Web browsers has changed the concept of the interface and proprietary systems are gradually being abandoned in favour of generic browser software. A single interface can provide access to the catalogue, Intranet and Internet facilities in a seamless way. Systems have already been developed for libraries that can search a catalogue and generate the results as HTML pages, providing a list of items which can be clicked on for further details. The use of JAVA and ACTIVEX will increase the ability of OPACs to offer more customized searching and a more personalized interaction with the library system.

☐ Libraries should work towards the provision of an integrated interface for users to search for information of all kinds.

Network developments
Increasing bandwidth

The demand for increased bandwidth for communications is insatiable. The Internet is already so overcrowded with data traffic that it is in danger of breaking down. The development of telephone audio transmission and video transmission over the Internet represents a massive increase in traffic which requires a much greater bandwidth than the traditional text-based traffic. Internet service providers are constantly increasing the bandwidth of their backbone supplies to keep up with the demand. Research has already started on Internet 2, the next generation of

Internet provision. The SuperJANET network which links academic institutions in the UK provides an example of the kind of network likely to be seen in the future.

Internally, the development of 100 Mb/s ethernet is providing organizations with improved bandwidth for multimedia networking. Video conferencing will become more common as bandwidth increases. Users will be able to request face-to-face interviews with library staff from remote terminals.

☐ Libraries will need to ensure that their networks are capable of dealing with a constantly increasing demand for bandwidth.

Increasing connections

The interconnection of computers on the Internet has provided a model for open networking. The rapid development of the Internet is now being matched by the connection of computers on internal networks and Intranets. With the advent of smaller and cheaper servers it is not unlikely that many individuals will eventually be connected to the Internet in the same way that organizations are now. Many Internet users have their own personal Web pages stored by their Internet service providers. It is only a small step to have a home computer acting as a server on the Internet and many small enterprises will use this as a means of doing business in the future.

Libraries have an opportunity to lead the way in developing services for their users across networks. As library staff develop the skills needed to introduce and maintain these services there is an opportunity for them to take the lead in their organization in developing IT systems. Libraries are often at the cutting edge of IT developments since their main activities are concerned with information retrieval and provision. Many university libraries have merged with computer departments in recognition that the campus network is the vital backbone of the organization.

Commercial organizations have evolved in a different way. The traditional library or information unit has never been a central part of the business function and IT systems have often developed out of data processing sections. Many information units, however, have seen the chance to extend their influence through the development of IT networking of CD-ROMs. The expertise gained in using the Internet can also be useful in setting up Intranets.

☐ Libraries will be expected to have servers accessible via the Internet.

☐ Libraries will be expected to provide access to the Internet as a routine service.

☐ Library and information staff can provide the necessary skills to organize the internal information resources of the parent organization.

Communication developments
Increasing methods

Every new communication device increases communication rather than replacing what existed before. Some systems such as the telegraph and telex have been superseded but there are many more devices now available. People have become used to telephones, cellular telephones, radio, fax, pagers, e-mail and more recently file transfer over the Internet. In the near future there will be further methods of communication employed including voice messaging, video conferencing and video phones, remote access to desktop computers and a variety of services developed from these methods. Some libraries have already experimented with video conferencing using ISDN connections and many large companies now use video routinely.

☐ Libraries must be prepared to provide a wider range of communication facilities in the future, allowing users to communicate more effectively with the library, with each other and with the external world.

Increasing information

The increasing volume of information has already been mentioned. The amount of printed information is still growing as more books are published each year. This will inevitably begin to decline as the impact of the growing trend towards electronic publishing continues.

The information society is a society that will be dependent upon information and so the amount of information generated is bound to increase further. This is particularly so with the advent of the

Internet and the concept of personal Web publishing. Individuals can now make information available for others in a way never before possible. Although much of this information is banal and of limited appeal there is no doubt that it will continue to grow in volume. Some attempts have already been made by librarians to provide help to Internet users by assembling useful lists of links for searching such as those specific to particular subjects.

☐ Libraries may not need in the long term to plan for ever-increasing storage of physical materials.
☐ Libraries will need to consider the most effective ways of helping their users navigate through the mass of electronic information available to them.
☐ Librarians and information workers could help users by developing better information retrieval tools based upon a knowledge of user preferences.

Increasing traffic

As the number of methods of communication increase and the amount of information grows so the traffic across networks will multiply. Congestion will become a constant problem. Dependency on a single network for all activities in a library is risky. The main internal network activity used to be the issue and discharge of books at different service points; this function now has to compete with others such as information retrieval from CD-ROMs. In the future multimedia services will add significantly to the traffic on networks with a consequent effect upon response times.

☐ Libraries should consider the lifespan of existing cable and if necessary include a replacement schedule to upgrade their networks as part of their future strategy.

Media developments
Increasing range

CD-ROMs have now become fairly standard as a portable storage medium for data. Software is now generally distributed on CD-ROM rather than floppy disk. Multimedia reference works and bibliographic databases are available in this format. Re-writeable

CD-ROM disks are now available as an alternative to floppy disks, holding over 400 times more data. In-house CD-ROM production using cheap writing devices is also possible for small runs of disks such as copying a library catalogue for wider distribution. Smaller CD-ROM disks are being produced by some manufacturers as an alternative to floppy disks. DVD disks, designed for storing more than two hours of continuous video, will also be useful for increased data storage and may allow individuals to carry their own data stores from one computer to another in the future. PCM-CIA cards developed for laptop computers have become increasingly sophisticated and may offer an alternative form of storage for programs and data for desktop machines in the future. Newer floppy disks and removable hard disks also complicate the picture.

Libraries are never likely to be pioneers in the use of new media but must judge what is most effective for their own use from those available. Publishers will inevitably dictate the form in which information is published and libraries must be prepared to accommodate a wide range of electronic media. Many terminals now have CD-ROM drives as standard but it is unlikely that every new medium can be accommodated in this way. Some media may have to be avoided altogether as decisions have to be made on which devices are most cost effective, user friendly and easy to maintain.

☐ Libraries will need to consider the loan of a wider range of electronic media to users in the future.
☐ Libraries may also have to make provision on their networks for devices that can read the new media at convenient points.

Increasing digitization

Print will be increasingly bypassed by many publishers who will put information directly on to the Internet as a means of cutting costs and gaining more effective control of the use of their products. Publishers of large, detailed information sources such as directories, bibliographic databases, commercial catalogues, statistics, patents and other documents which have only ever been marginally economic in printed form are migrating to the Internet. As access security problems are overcome and electronic charging mechanisms are perfected more information will be available in this way, possibly only in this way. A premium may be charged for production in print or some other medium. The question of whether or not libraries should recharge users for downloading information that has to be paid for by the byte will need to be debated.

☐ Libraries will increasingly find themselves in the role of gateways to external systems, providing access to information over which they have no ownership rights and little control.
☐ Libraries may find some products becoming too expensive to acquire in a physical format and may need to consider subscriptions to Internet-based services for their users as an alternative.

Increasing definition

Digital information can provide much greater definition than older analogue information. Images can be sharper and more detailed. The quality of multimedia is increasing. Video, virtual reality and sound systems are all improving. Commercial systems will set the trend for what is acceptable. As the definition increases the quality of production comes under greater scrutiny. The trend towards amateur production of video and images typified by the results of camcorder and digital camera images displayed on Web pages demonstrates how easy it is to produce poor-quality results with hi-tech equipment. The trend towards multimedia will throw up new learning challenges for librarians.

☐ Librarians will need to develop new skills in developing and using multimedia facilities.

Social trends
Increasing learning

People are living longer and studying and learning for a greater proportion of their lives. The need for information does not necessarily diminish as people get older. At present the trend in many organizations is for earlier retirement or redundancy and the average age of employees is decreasing. Many people now expect to have more than one career during their lifetime. The demand for education and information is likely to increase. Demands upon libraries may increase or at least remain constant despite the increasing competition from other sources of information and entertainment. Whether older people require different library services is hard to say but they are likely to be more demanding in the future. Future users will be more computer literate, having been educated in an environment in which computers are ubiquitous. The introduction of hole-in-the-wall machines in banks was originally derided in the belief that people wanted personal service above all else. In fact, the opposite was true and it is noticeable that queues form outside machines at banks even when there are staff available to deal with transactions. In future, it is likely that a generation raised on computer games and PCs will go to terminals first and foremost for information rather than library staff.

☐ Libraries will need to provide more facilities for self-learning in future.

☐ Libraries will need to provide more terminals for a generation of computer-literate users.

Increasing population

The world's population continues to grow and the demand upon material resources becomes greater. Increased competition for resources will accelerate the use of IT systems for communication as travel to work and business is increasingly seen as wasteful. Teleworking, telecommuting and telelearning will increase.

☐ Libraries will have to provide services for remote users who will not wish to visit a physical site for information.

Increasing competition

The range of leisure activities continues to grow. With more television channels available through cable networks and a variety of interactive services appearing, there is increased competition for the time people once spent reading books. Alternative information services will continue to appear as the possibilities of electronic systems are explored. Users will increasingly prefer to obtain information from their home computers linked into external networks. Visits to libraries may seem inconvenient by comparison.

☐ Libraries must be able to offer something more than can be obtained by users at home.

☐ Libraries will need to market their services effectively to attract users away from alternative information providers.

Copyright and intellectual property
Increasing restrictions

Attempts have been made recently to introduce greater restrictions upon copyright and intellectual property. There is likely to be an increasing movement towards further controls on the copying of electronic media. The Internet provides an ideal medium for people to copy, download and reuse text and images. Copyright in this area has not yet been clarified but it is likely that the present free-for-all will come under increasing control. Libraries already have an obligation to monitor photocopying to ensure that users comply with the law.

☐ Libraries may have to develop methods of policing what their users are downloading.

Commercial information providers
Increasing charges

As businesses, publishers seek to maximize their profits. One way of doing this may be to cut production costs by ceasing to publish in printed form. Some business information publishers have announced their intention to move on to the Internet where the cost of maintaining a database is lower than producing printed directories. Access can be restricted by password to bona fide subscribers who can then be billed for each access or download they make. Eventually this system could apply to many other types of information. The increasing commercialization of the Internet will bring with it increased costs for libraries and individuals.

☐ Libraries may have to become used to the idea of paying for access to electronic information on behalf of their users rather than buying physical stock.

Increasing publishers

Electronic information is relatively cheap to produce compared to traditional print and other media. Individuals can set themselves up as amateur publishers and publish to the world on the Internet. The number of purely electronic publications is increasing. E-zines or electronic magazines now appear in many forms. Some are distributed via e-mail, others are made available on the Web. Many other publications are prepared for the Internet first rather than print. The cost of desktop publishing has also decreased and short runs of specialized publications have become more economically viable. CD-ROMs can be produced relatively cheaply in short runs using inexpensive CD players that can write on to blank discs. The number of titles in print continues to rise, although print runs for each title have become smaller. This proliferation of publishing may present problems for libraries in the future, as well as adding to the confusion of users in finding the information they require. There will be an increasing need to help users find their way through this maze of information.

☐ Libraries should consider the development of electronic guides for their users.

Personal access
Increasing points of access

The trend towards access to information through terminals will not be restricted to libraries. Kiosk terminals are beginning to appear in public places, providing tourist information and local community information. There is likely to be a proliferation of such terminals in the future. At the same time there are moves towards making electronic information available through such things as cellular phones and pagers, laptop and pocket computers, PDAs and other devices. The domestic market is being targeted with Internet television, interactive cable and digital television, all of which are potential information providers. This will add to the competition for libraries.

☐ Libraries may need to provide remote access to their networks through a variety of technologies.
☐ Libraries may face demands for such devices to be made available for users.

Information society trends
Increasing globalization

The Internet provides near universal access. Putting a Web page on the Internet for a small group of users also opens up an organization to the world. There may be unexpected consequences of doing this. A library may end up spending a good deal of time dealing with enquiries from outsiders who are not its natural users. Enquiries will be received from different countries by e-mail. People will use the opportunity of communicating with the library via the Internet in order to obtain information from within the library. Manchester Public Library's Web page has stimulated e-mail enquiries from many different countries, mainly for local history or genealogical information. People will increasingly contact the library they think will best deal with their enquiry regardless of its geographical location.

Many libraries have unique collections which could be made available to a global audience if the texts or the images were digitized. There are a number of digitization programmes already being undertaken by national libraries and other bodies such as Project Gutenberg which has already produced thousands of electronic versions of classic novels and standard works. This work is expensive for individual libraries and in many cases would require external funding.

☐ Libraries will need to design policies to deal with enquiries from global users.
☐ Libraries that have special collections will need to consider how they can provide global access to their unique resources.

Increasing intrusion

IT is increasingly being used for security purposes. Surveillance cameras linked via ISDN lines to central control units can detect movement and automatically summon security personnel. The increasing value of IT equipment and the need to protect investments against theft and vandalism will demand greater security.

The use of IT systems can be logged in detail at every terminal on a network. In future bona fide users may be given smartcards to gain access to buildings and equipment. Some university libraries are already experimenting with such systems. Buildings in the future will be smarter and will be able to monitor the movements of users. Data collected in this way may be used for more effective management but there are issues of intrusion to be considered. Some organizations have a policy of openness about the use of security cameras and videotapes and publish guidelines about their use. Others regard security as a private issue.

Many libraries have had to adopt policies concerning access to pornographic material on the Internet. Some guidelines for public access to the Internet in libraries have been published on special Web pages in the USA. Some model disclaimers of legal liability for libraries are also available for perusal. At the same time there are a number of groups working against the increasing censorship of information on the Internet.

☐ Libraries will need to be aware of the sensitive issues involved in this area and may need to determine policies to protect themselves and their patrons.
☐ Libraries may need to develop policies concerning the collection and use of information about their users.

Consequences for libraries
Increasing demands

The introduction of more IT systems generally means an increase in the range of services offered by libraries. IT rarely offers a straightforward substitution for non-IT tasks and facilities. Old and new systems may have to be run in parallel for some time. Even when an IT system supersedes a manual one it may demand almost as much work to maintain as its predecessor. The expansion of services and the consequent need for a wider range of skills among library and information staff places extra burdens upon the library service which are likely to increase further in the future. The rapid changes taking place in IT means that there will be a need to devote more and more time to training. Each new facility opens up a new world of possibilities. The Internet alone can require knowledge of e-mail, listservers, World Wide Web, search engines, HTML, cgi, ftp, Telnet, IRC, JAVA and dozens of other programs, plug-ins and protocols. The jargon alone requires extensive study.

☐ Libraries will need to devote more time and effort to training in IT skills in the future.

Increasing expectations

Some IT projects may place the library service in the spotlight for the first time. A Web page on the Internet, for example, opens up the library service to the critical scrutiny of the world. An organization can easily become judged by the quality and content of its pages and a poor impression may damage the reputation of the library service. There will be increasing pressures to produce a professional-looking product which will require effective resourcing. A library service may in future be judged by its IT facilities. The expectations of users will be based upon what is available on networks elsewhere and libraries may be competing against commercial organizations with far greater resources.

☐ Libraries must learn to compete effectively with other organizations if they are to survive in the future.

Increasing dependence

More and more library functions are being translated from manual systems into IT systems and the completely automated library cannot be ruled out. In the meantime there will be a gradual introduction of self-issuing systems, more sophisticated and intelligent catalogues, more convenient electronic delivery of information and more terminal-based activity. The majority of organizations will become increasingly dependent upon IT systems. Many already cannot function without them and there is unlikely to be a reduction in this dependency in the future. Once this concept has been accepted there is no reason why it should be of any more concern than dependency upon electricity or the telephone.

☐ Libraries must commit themselves wholeheartedly to the increasing use of IT in the future and develop strategies to make the best use of IT for their users.

References

1   Fromm, Erich, *The sane society*, Ch. 9, 1955.

Appendix 1 IT strategy checklist

Aims and scope of the strategy
☐ establish the aims of the strategy
☐ obtain senior management support
☐ set up a steering group
☐ define the limits of the strategy
☐ set up a strategy team
☐ obtain the resources to carry out the work.

Internal audit
☐ obtain an overview of the overall management strategy
☐ include plans for information management
☐ assess user and organizational needs
☐ undertake an IT audit
☐ assess human assets for IT development
☐ assess physical assets and liabilities of buildings etc.

The external context
☐ examine external threats and opportunities
☐ assess pressures for change from external bodies
☐ examine the state of the art in IT
☐ look at practice in other libraries and information services
☐ gather information through research, visits and workshops
☐ identify the main development aims.

Elements of the strategy – physical infrastructure
☐ assess the need for networks, hardware, software etc.
☐ look at the potential of different media and online facilities
☐ examine broadband services
☐ examine the library's role as an electronic information provider
☐ produce an infrastructure plan for the library service.

Elements of the strategy - policy and management

☐ develop policies for IT
☐ look at the management of future IT systems and support
☐ consider the training implications of IT
☐ consider improvements to management efficiency
☐ consider the budgeting implications of IT
☐ look at partnerships with other libraries and organizations
☐ consider security.

Evaluation and implementation

☐ evaluate strategy plans before detailed implementation
☐ develop implementation plans
☐ consider the problems of implementing large systems
☐ look at alternatives for financing IT development
☐ plan staffing for implementation
☐ produce specifications for tender
☐ plan for installation and testing
☐ plan staff training
☐ consider risks.

Monitoring and review

☐ plan monitoring activities
☐ measure benefits of new IT facilities
☐ continue to monitor external developments
☐ plan the review process
☐ deal with failures.

Future strategy for libraries

☐ develop flexible IT strategies that can adapt to change
☐ develop an awareness of future IT developments that might affect library IT strategies
☐ consider social changes and their possible impact on library and information services.

Appendix 2 Further reading

Budgeting

Snyder, Herbert and Davenport, Elisabeth, *Costing and pricing in the digital age: a practical guide for information services*, London, Library Association Publishing, 1997.

Networking

Dyson, Peter, *Dictionary of networking*, San Francisco, Sybex, 2nd edn, 1995.

MaNamara, John E., *Local area networks an introduction to the technology*, Boston, Digital Press, 2nd edn, 1996.

Dempsey, Lorcan, Law, Derek and Mowat, Ian, *Networking and the future of libraries 2: managing the intellectual record: an International Conference held at the University of Bath 19–21 April 1995*, London, Library Association Publishing, 1996 (hbk), 1997 (pbk).

IT audit

Chambers, Andrew D. and John M. Court, *Computer auditing*, London, Pitman, 3rd edn, 1991.

Strategy

Whittington, Richard, *What is strategy - and does it matter?*, London, Routledge, 1993.

Luffman, George and others, *Strategic management*, Oxford, Blackwell, 3rd edn, 1996.

IT strategy

Tozer, Edwin E., *Strategic IS/IT planning*, London, Butterworth-Heinemann, 1996.

Boar, Bernard, *Strategic thinking for information technology: how to build the IT organization for the information age*, New York,

Wiley, 1997.

Feeny, David etc. (ed.), *Managing information technology as a strategic resource*, London, McGraw, 1997.

Information technology management: IT management handbook, London, Butterworth-Heinemann, 1992.

Currie, Wendy, *Management strategy for information technology*, London, Pitman, 1995.

Information society

National Information Infrastructure, *The administration's agenda for action*, 1995.
  http://sunsite.unc.edu/nii/NII-Agenda-for-Action.htm

Bangeman, Martin., *Europe and the global information society, Recommendations to the European Council*, Brussels, European Commission, 26 May 1994.
  http://www.ispo.cec.be/infosoc/backg/bangeman.html

European Commission, *Europe's way to the information society: an action plan*. COM(94) 347, Final. Brussels, European Commission, 1994.
  http://www.ispo.cec.be/infosoc/backg/action.html

ISPO, *Studies and publications on the Information Society*, 1997.
  http://www.ispo.cec.be/infosoc/promo/pubs.html

Sample IT strategy statements

Moffett, J., *An information technology strategy document*, Ashmolean IT report 1, 1995.
  http://www.ashmol.ox.ac.uk/ash/itdevel/amitr1.html

Anglia Polytechnic University, *An IT strategy for Anglia Polytechnic University 1996–2001*, 1995.
  http://bridge.anglia.ac.uk/fes/computer/itstrat.htm

Index